Freedom to Publish

Freedom to Publish

*A report on obstacles to freedom in
publishing prepared for the Congress of
the International Publishers Association,
Stockholm, May 1980*

by

Peter Calvocoressi

assisted by Ann Bristow

Writers and Scholars Educational Trust
and Index on Censorship

Foreword by
Winthrop Knowlton

K
3255
.C34x
West

Published for
International Publishers Association

by

ALMQVIST & WIKSELL INTERNATIONAL
Stockholm – Sweden

HUMANITIES PRESS　　　　INDEX ON CENSORSHIP
N.J. · USA　　　　　　　　LONDON · ENGLAND

© 1980 by the International Publishers Association
All rights reserved
ISBN 91-22-00361-4
First published in Sweden 1980 by
Almqvist & Wiksell International, Stockholm

in collaboration with
Humanities Press Inc., Atlantic Highlands, N.J. 07716, U.S.A.
ISBN 0-391-01949-X

and

Index on Censorship, London, England
ISBN 0-904286-22-3

Foreword

Since the last Congress of the International Publishers Association was held in Kyoto in May, 1976 the I PA's International Freedom to Publish Committee, under my chairmanship, has been engaged in the task of surveying the state of freedom of expression in member countries.

As a first step, a detailed questionnaire was developed by the committee, with valuable help from our secretariat, and mailed to member associations in more than 40 countries. Approximately half the membership responded.

The committee then comissioned Writers & Scholars International Ltd., the publishers of INDEX Magazine, to take this data, to analyze it, and to supplement it with their own knowledge of and experience in these matters—all this with the objective of presenting to our committee a report which, in turn, we could submit to the Stockholm Congress in May of 1980 for review and discussion by the membership at large. Writers & Scholars commissioned Peter Calvocoressi, a distinguished British publisher, to undertake the task on their behalf, and his efforts our committee now presents to you in the form of this report.

We believe Mr. Calvocoressi has done a brilliant job. The report is thorough, eloquent, measured—and we think it will be a valuable basis for discussion—and perhaps action—in Stockholm. Nothing quite like it has been written before. It does not limit itself to "political" restraints on freedom of expression but to practical and cultural and financial restraints as well. It does not "pull any punches" but its tone is neither strident nor polemical: it is wise and humane. We are grateful for his work.

Having identified a number of obstacles to freedom to publishing in our member countries, Mr. Calvocoressi concludes "that outside the world's avowed ideological and military autocracies, freedom to publish is widespread but vulnerable." It is this committee's keen hope that the delegates will read his report in Stockholm so that, in good spirit and sensitive to the precious quality of the freedoms we enjoy, we can address ourselves to these questions: Are the obstacles described the most *important* ones? What are our responsibilities as publishers in removing them. What are the likely prospects for doing so? Can we improve these prospects by working together—within countries and across borders, as an international association? If so, what specifically should we do? And when should we begin?

I wish to conclude this brief introduction by thanking my committee members for their dedication and hard work during this four year period—Ian Chapman, William Collins, Sons & Co., England; Brikt Jensen, Gyldendal Norsk Forlag, Norway; Jean-Jacques Nathan, Fernand Nathan Editeur, France; Per A. Sjögren (President, IPA), Raben & Sjögren Bokförlag, Sweden. We have held meetings during this period in Paris, London, Moscow, San Francisco, Frankfurt, and New York. We have tried to conduct our deliberations in a manner consistent with the aims of the Association's charter, which states:

Freedom of thought, expressed both in speech and print, is the mainspring of the spiritual life of man and of his mental activity. Without that freedom the whole of literature—the recorded fruits of that activity—would suffer to the detriment of human growth in character and in knowledge. All, therefore, who understand the value of freedom of thought, speech and writing, and especially publishers, should unite to maintain that freedom, and firmly to oppose any attempts to restrict it.

The International Publishers Association has the essential task of upholding and defending the right of publishers complete freedom, provided they respect all legal rights attached to these works both within the frontiers of each country and among nations. Its duty is to oppose steadfastly any attempt of threat to restrict that freedom. The International Publishers Associatoin considers that its duty is also to overcome illiteracy and the lack of books and of other educational materials.

Respectfully submitted,
Winthrop Knowlton

Contents

Introduction

I was commissioned a year ago by Writers and Scholars Educational Trust to prepare for the International Publishers Association a report on the obstacles to freedom in publishing with particular reference to those parts of the world where the IPA has constituent Associations. I accepted this task the more willingly since the subject has a profound importance, not merely for publishers and publishing, but also for the liberal cultures and values which publishers have helped to fashion ever since their emergence at the time of the invention of printing.

As a first step towards the production of this report the I PA sent a questionnaire to its 42 member Associations. Half of them replied and half did not. I have found some of the replies more helpful than others. This basic material has provided me with a sample rather than a survey of publishers' views and problems.

My principal problem has been to supplement this information within the time and the budgetary provision available to me. My task would have been impossible without the help given me by Ann Bristow, to whose industry and percipience this report is greatly indebted. I am also indebted to Michael Scammell, the Director of Writers and Scholars Educational Trust, and to Jenny Pearce, the Trust's Latin American specialist, for information which they gleaned in the course of two separate visits to parts of Latin America; to other members of the Trust's staff for expert background knowledge put at my disposal; and to Blaine Stothard for valuable information and comment.

I wish to emphasise that this report rests upon information from a restricted number of countries. It is not a comprehensive catalogue of the varying situations which exist in the world or even in that part of the world where the I PA has members. On the other hand it is, I believe, a reasonably comprehensive survey of the problems which confront publishers who are worried about the freedom to publish. In making this survey I have sought to illustrate these problems as widely as possible, using the answers to the I PA's questionnaires, supplementary research and my own experience in publishing in the years 1959–63 and 1972–76.

Censorship is an exercise of power or prejudice. The power may be political or financial. It may be exercised by the state with which the first four chapters of this report are mainly concerned, or by private organisations. The prejudice, whether benign or malign, derives from society's inherited conventions demanding conformity in the name either of a moral imperative or of a majority. The general tenor of my inquiry into these matters is that outside the world's avowed ideological and military autocracies, freedom to publish is widespread but vulnerable.

Peter Calvocoressi
September 1979

1. The Censor

The censor is a discredited but not extinct being. Every autocrat is a censor at heart and every paternalist hankers after the censor's powers. But progress from more authoritarian to more open and more liberal societies undermines the censor who ceases to be the honoured custodian of moral standards and good behaviour and becomes instead a repressive symbol of power and prejudice. Chief among the reasons for this reversal of repute has been the censor's interference with freedom of speech and the written word.

In his pure form the censor exercises a pre-publication veto. Restraints of this kind, although common in Communist countries, are now so generally regarded as obnoxious outside them that even military and ideological autocracies feel compelled to justify their use as emergency measures only. Much commoner is a second kind of censorship under which publications do not require an official imprimatur but are banned after publication. A book's author, publisher, printer or distributor—and normally all of these—may then be prosecuted because the book presents to the public what the law says may not be presented or what the executive power, regardless of the letter of the law, wishes to suppress. Censorship of this kind is formally indistinguishable from prosecution for breach of the criminal law, or from naked executive repression.

The term censorship is also used in the misleading phrase

self-censorship—misleading because self-censorship is not necessarily a free act or decision. Self-censorship is commonly brought into play when authority creates a situation in which it is dangerous for the publisher not to censor his own publication. By creating this situation authority forces the publisher, author etc. to do the job which authority shrinks from doing too openly. Authority hopes in this way to achieve its repressive aims with a minimum of odium.

Pure or pre-publication censorship requires the creation of agencies to which books must be submitted before they may be printed. These are rare outside avowed autocracies.

India — Israel

Censorship was imposed in India during the recent Emergency by the Prevention of Publication of Objectionable Matter Act and by regulations under the Defence of India Act. These were repealed when the Emergency was deemed to be over. In Israel, a state at war, books affecting national security have to be submitted in advance of publication to military censorship. The army has quarters in the Press House at Tel Aviv where officers read such books and pronounce upon them. The publisher may appeal to a civilian court against a military veto, but such an appeal never succeeds. The courts believe that the military know best. The system works smoothly because authors and publishers do not try to challenge or evade it: they accept it as a necessary consequence of the state of war. There is the occasional borderline case. One such was Mati Golan's book on Kissinger's shuttle diplomacy in the Middle East. This was published without reference to the censor although it was held by many to fall within the system. The author remains in government service.

In its occupied territories Israel has deployed wider powers of suppression, banning the import into the territories of venomous Arab literature. The authorities decide what is venomous.

Indonesia

Similar control over imports, as distinct from domestic publication, is exercised in Indonesia where Presidential Decree 4 requires foreign books to be submitted in advance and gives the government power to exclude any which may be harmful to Indonesian society and the Indonesian revolution. Most of the books kept out in this way have been in English, but in 1978 all imports of books from China were stopped. The appearance of Amnesty International's report on Indonesia in a Jakarta bookshop shows that the system does not always work as might be expected.

Indonesian publishers do not require a licence for each book printed within the country, but they are required to be themselves licensed as publishers by the Ministry of Information. Until 1977 KOPKAMTIB (Command for the Restoration of Security and Order) also issued printing licences but these are no longer compulsory. Both the federal Attorney General and local authorities may ban books but only after publication.

Although the present regime in Indonesia took power as long ago as 1965 it has seen itself for many of these years as embattled—like Israel. Presumably Noor Mohammed Taraki had a similar sense of emergency when in 1979 he required Afghanistan's author-publishers (the two occupations are combined in that country) to seek official consent before putting their writings into print. When no such emergency can be pleaded most countries not only eschew pre-publication censorship but go to the lengths of condemning it in formal and solemn manner by listing in their constitutions whole series of freedoms, among which the freedom to publish is prominent. The language of these guarantees is strikingly alike, but the results are not. There is a problem of appearance and reality, to which we come when we consider post-publication censorship.

Freedom to publish is nowhere absolute and the most numerous limitations upon it are imposed by the law. Thus national security requires that certain matters be kep secret (see the next chapter). Many countries prohibit, in their constitutional or general laws, statements inciting racial violence or religious hatred or lauding aggressive war. The law also frequently prohibits the publication of obscene matter (either generally or to children) or the introduction of subversive or pacifist matter into military establishments. And the transgressing of these and similar restrictions may be followed by criminal proceedings. This is censorship *post hoc*. It co-exists with guarantees of freedom and fluctuates with governmental purposes and the political climate. Much of it is unobjectionable or is held by a majority to be so. But since the law is, by its nature, general and in that sense imprecise, such restrictions on freedom are open to political manipulation and mean different things in different settings.

Brazil – Norway

The Brazilian constitution of 1969 states in article 153 that "the publication of books... requires no licence from authority." It then restricts this fundamental freedom by prohibiting—in terms common throughout much of the world—war prop-

18

aganda, attacks on public order and religious beliefs, race or class propaganda, and publications contrary to morals and good behaviour. Similarly in Norway the constitution provides that "no person may be punished for any writing, no matter its contents, which he may cause to be printed or published, unless he wilfully and demonstrably either personally induced or encouraged others to disobey the laws or show disrespect for religion or morals... or uttered false and defamatory accusations..."

Here are two admirable—and typical—constitutional guarantees, each of them hedged about with conditions which, on the face of them, are not superficially unacceptable. But since the conditions are necessarily couched in general terms, what happens in practice depends on how the authorities, executive or judicial, interpret the limiting clauses. Judged by their constitutional appearances Brazil and Norway are very much alike. But this has not been so.

In Brazil the existence of the constitutional guarantee has proved compatible with laws and decrees of a very different tenor, under which the regime of freedom promised by the constitution has been overlaid by its opposite. There are indications, as this report is being written, that things are changing. In June 1978 censorship was authoritatively denounced and a year later, at a meeting in Rio de Janeiro of the International PEN Club, uninhibited attacks on censorship were made in the presence of the newly installed President Figuieredo. The announcement of a substantial, if not total, amnesty of political prisoners is another indication of a changing climate, but the uncertainties in the situation were emphasized by two events in May 1979. On the one hand General Hugo Abreu was sentenced to 20 days' imprisonment (a curiously and perhaps indicatively short term) for publishing his *Oltro Lado do Poder* (The Other Side of Power), which criticised the autocratic way in which the new President had been chosen. On the other hand Fernando Pacheco Jordão was allowed to publish a full account of the notorious imprisonment and murder of the Brazilian journalist Vladimir Herzog: the book was twice reprinted. Two months later, in July, Carlos Fon, who had already been charged for writing about police torture in a popular magazine, was able to publish without hindrance a book on the same subject.

But whatever the future may hold, the past presents an object lesson in how censorship may flourish in spite of the most explicit guarantees against it.

The Brazilian military dictatorship, which was inaugurated by the coup of 1964 and remains in being to this day, imposed at the end of 1968 Institutional Act No. 5 which became an instrument for the extensive repression of institutions, civil rights, individuals and books. It authorised, among other things, the burning of books and proceedings by court martial. A year later the dictatorship introduced in addition Decree Law No. 1077, directed ostensibly against sexual promiscuity and the undermining of sound morality but capable of being used as a catch-all weapon against whatever official caprice chose to consider a danger to the state. Edict No. 427 of 1977 imposed censorship of imported books.

Institutional Act No. 5 was repealed in 1978 when the dictatorship set about giving itself a milder face but it has been replaced by a National Security Law (1979) which makes it a crime: to disseminate in any form or for any reason propaganda material from foreign sources intended to undermine "national doctrines" or to implant ideas incompatible with the constitution; to disseminate by any medium false or "tendentious" information, or true facts in an "incomplete or misleading" manner, in such a way as to incite or try to incite people against the "constitutional authorities"; to insult publicly by

20

word or writing the head of a foreign government or nation; to permit the use of communications media for the execution of a "crime against national security"; and to create subversive propaganda by means of (*inter alia*) books. These offences and others equally imprecise may be visited with terms of imprisonment and the Minister of Justice is empowered, without recourse to judicial procedures, to seize books, prevent their publication and prohibit their circulation and distribution. Since the beginning of 1979 therefore it would seem that pre- as well as post-publication censorship by executive, non-judicial act is permitted within terms so broad that the Minister of Justice is virtually a law unto himself.

In the last fifteen years Brazilian publishers and writers have had to choose between rigorous self-censorship, going to gaol or fleeing the country. It is impossible to catalogue the full tale of woe. Several hundred books have been banned. A few cases have received international attention and are cited here as examples of what can happen in a country where the constitution forbids pre-publication censorship but laws of various kinds have been used to enable the government, whether by prosecuting the few or intimidating the many, to prevent the publication of whatever it does not like.

Em Camera Lento (In Slow Motion), a novel with a political message by Renato Tapajos, was banned and its author gaoled—the book has, however, recently been relieved from the ban. Another novel, *Feliz Ano Novo (Happy New Year)* by Rubem Fonseca, was banned after having been on sale for eight months. *Zero* by Ignatius de Loyola Brandão, published in 1975, was suppressed the next year. *Aracelli, Meu Amor (Aracelli, My Love)* by José Luzeiro, a fictionalized account of the rape of a poor girl by a number of rich boys, was burned by ministerial decree not without suspicion that the Minister had been got at by the boys' influential parents. *A Ditadura dos*

21

Carteis (The Dictatorship of the Trusts) by Kurt Mirow, an attack on the secret machinations of multi-national corporations in Brazil, was subjected to prosecution on grounds of national security but in this case the author was acquitted. Finally, a new history of Brazil, regarded by the government as too left wing or marxist in its interpretations, was ordered to be burnt. There is nothing in the new National Security Law to prevent further cases of this kind. The Brazilian publisher's freedom to publish still depends more upon the climate created by authority than on the letter of the law.

Argentina

In Argentina, where article 14 of the (unrevoked) constitution guarantees freedom of expression, the military regime which seized power in 1976 has avoided the introduction of pre-publication censorship by achieving its repressive aims by other means. There was immediate and wholesale destruction of books. In Córdoba, for example, the army ordered all bookshops and bookstalls to eliminate all "subversive" material in 24 hours, and the next day large numbers of books were seized and burnt. Similar action was taken in Buenos Aires and elsewhere. Booksellers were kidnapped and publishers forced to close; the influential Mexican publishers Siglo XXI were evicted from the country, their entire output branded subversive and some of their staff arrested. Left wing literature, from the works of Marx and Lenin to whatever the government chooses to condemn, has been banned and this ban has been upheld in some quarters on the patently absurd pretext that nobody wants to read such books any more. The regime's intolerance extends to Roman Catholic publishers who have specialized in the problems of underdeveloped countries and in what Latin Americans call the "theology of liberation". Books are referred to a commission which may decide either to ban them outright or to allow them to be stocked and sold but not displayed. Banning decrees are published and are enforced by official inspections of bookshops or, outside Buenos Aires, by the more happy-go-lucky visitations of the local police. Banning decrees have become less numerous since publishers have themselves cut their publishing and restricted their imports in order to escape official displeasure. They have even been intimidated into rejecting books which they might, with a little more nerve, publish with impunity.

Bolivia

An equally stark illustration of the irrelevance of laws and constitutions in the face of executive determination is provided by Bolivia where, under the rule of General Hugo Banzer up to 1978, what mattered was the President's will. Books critical of him could neither be published nor imported and writers whom he did not like were exiled or harassed. Thus in 1972 the entire edition of *Guerilla Blanca dentro de Masas Indias* by Ramiro Reynaga Burgao, an analysis of Latin American society from an Indian point of view, was seized in the author's mother's flat in La Paz. The author, a former president of the law faculty of La Paz University, had been in exile since 1967 but his mother, aged 70, and other relatives were arrested. (Bolivian writers have also to contend with the fact that one third of the population cannot read and there are only two considerable publishers. A book which sells 1,000 copies is a best seller.)

Uruguay

In Uruguay marxist ideas have been declared "dangerous" and the mere possession of marxist literature is proof of belief in such ideas. Since the coup of 1972 a number of authors have been harassed, e.g. the poet Cristina Peri Rossi and Mario Benedetti, a popular writer and socialist admirer of Fidel Castro. The old established publishers Arca, Alfa and Marcha, well known for their editions of serious works in economics, psychology and sociology (including translations of the Frankfurt school), have been forced to go out of business. Publishers and booksellers have had menacing visits from the police. The number of books published has halved.

East Germany

An ingenious ruse has been used by the East German government in an attempt to stretch censorship beyond the borders of the state. When Stefan Heym published his novel *Collin* in West Germany, the East German government fined him on the grounds that this publication was a violation of the law regarding foreign currency.

Czechoslovakia – USSR

In the same vein Czechoslovakia punitively taxes royalties derived from publication abroad, and in the USSR, where it is illegal to receive foreign currencies on any account, this ostensibly economic regulation is used—in the case of authors—to operate as a form of censorship.

Kenya – Haiti

Finally, we may note in this section the tendency of governments to ban books partly on account of the language in which they are written. This was the case with Ngugi wa Thiong'o whose work was allowed to appear unmolested in Kenya so long as it was in English but was banned as soon as Ngugi turned to a more widely understood language. Precisely the same consideration has guided President Duvalier in Haiti where books in Creole critical of his regime have been banned, although similar works in French—intelligible to only a tenth of the population—have not.

Further instances of post-publication censorship by government occur under the two broad categories of the defence of the state and the defence of morals, which are examined in chapters 2 and 3 of this report.

Self-censorship denotes the publisher's own refusal, dictated by prudence or timorousness, to publish a work which might bring a prosecution upon his head. Self-censorship is both a restraint on publication and an exercise of the publisher's personal freedom of choice. It is that choice tempered by a realization of the consequences of saying yes rather than no. In judging such self-censorship it is necessary to distinguish its sources. A publisher may, in the first place, refuse to publish a book because he does not like its message or its language. Although this judgment may be based on considerations not strictly literary or aesthetic, it cannot be argued that the publisher should not have this freedom of choice; and to that extent the term self-censorship is but dubiously appropriate to the case. But the publisher's refusal is as likely to be dictated by fear as by conviction—fear, that is to say, either of prosecution or other action (e.g. confiscation) by the state, or fear of social disapproval. Thus the publisher who acts as his own censor may be responding to his personal view of what is fit to publish, but alternatively he may be moved by fear of authority or by the social norms of his country and his class. Playing safe is sometimes the best—or only—way to stay in business. As one Mexican publisher put it: "It is better to work on the chessboard than off it.".

Many member Associations have reported that there is no self-censorship in their countries. It is, however, difficult to accept this view on any meaningful use of the term. So long as there are things which the law forbids or the government frowns on, or things which outrage society publishers will for the most part try to steer clear of trouble—from the law, from the powers that be, and from the social cold shoulder or snub. The possible troubles are diverse. They include penalties such as imprisonment and fines, the seizure and destruction of books by the police, and the indefinable but no less sensible consequences of transgressing commonly accepted, if ill defined, standards of propriety. In surveying these fields, where most people would accept that restraints do operate and even within limits should, the libertarian should keep one guiding principle in mind; that there is a sharp division between the self-censorship which arises from the publisher's own judgements or prejudices, and the self-censorship which is imposed or induced by external authority or pressures. Later sections of this report pay particular attention to this essential clog on publication—i.e. the limitations on a publisher's professional judgment, whether arising from the social ambience, the activities of pressure groups, or the loss of the publisher's independence to external proprietors and masters. We conclude this chapter with two observations.

First: the publisher falls into a dilemma whenever he accepts an obligation which diverges from the imperative of freedom which is—or should be—part of his stock-in-trade. For example, in Indonesia and elsewhere the publisher's freedom to publish has been made conditional upon his accepting a social and political role: he is to be an instrument of the revolution and a social agent, in terms which are set by the Government. Consequently his freedom must be exercised by him in certain ways and not in others. (Law II of 1966 and the Press Law partly spell out the conditions of his freedom.) He is turned into a compulsory self-censor as soon as he accepts this role as an imposed public duty and not as a matter of private conscience.

Second: self-censorship may have the effect of banning what an official censor would not ban. For example, in the aftermath of the civil war in Nigeria the authorities did not proscribe Wole Soyinka's prison notes *The Man Died* but one of his publishers did. The original hardcover edition of the book, published by Rex Collings, was freely distributed and sold in Nigeria. But when Penguin Books produced a paperback edition their proprietors, Pearsons, fearful for their other commitments in Nigeria, intervened and, even though a contract had been signed, prevented publication. The hardcover edition remained openly on sale and in demand.

2. The Defence of the State

There are two broad fields in which the state claims a right and a duty to curtail freedom of speech and publication in the public interest. These are the defence of the state itself, which is the subject of the present chapter, and the defence of morals and good behaviour, which will be considered in the next chapter.

The defence of the existence and integrity of the state is incontestably part of the business of government. It includes the defence of the state against external enemies and the pre-servation of public order against internal enemies. But within these categories questions arise about the nature and extent of permissible state action and, in particular, about the degree to which freedom of speech and publication may properly be sacrificed. Furthermore, the notion of the defence of the state has been widened in ways which are themselves questionable. These include the extension of the concept of the defence of the state to embrace not only its existence and integrity but also the protection of certain ideas or doctrines which are declared to be essential to its well-being, and the proscribing of others which are declared to be detrimental; and special measures for the protection of the state's dignitaries and symbols and the workings of its diplomacy.

The central issue in the defence of the state is the issue of secrecy. The state has secrets and needs to keep them. This proposition is very widely accepted. Hardly less widely accepted is the second proposition that in the last resort the state itself, through its executive officers, or its judiciary, must rule on what is a necessary secret and what is not. The corollary of these propositions is that governments are widely suspected of abusing them in order, not to defend the national interest, but to make government easier or from worse motives than that.

At the heart of this matter lies a fundamental conflict between opposed and irreconcilable views. While it is common ground that states have secrets and need justifiably to keep them, from this common ground different conclusions are drawn. On the one hand it is argued that only the state itself can know what revelations will be harmful to the nation and that therefore the state must be allowed, in the national interest, to control what may be published and what may not—either by pre-publication censorship or by post-publication indictment. The state is trusted, with varying degrees of willingness or unwillingness, to set the limits and monitor them. This view amounts in effect to a decision to give the preference to security over freedom in the inescapable conflict between the two. Security is paramount.

The opposing view reverses this judgment and makes the freedom to inquire and publish paramount. It denies the overriding claims of security and alleges that the health of the nation is more intimately bound up with freedom than with security. Consequently it advocates the widest access to information despite the risks to security implicit in this lifting of the guard on secrets. It does not go to the lengths of lifting the guard entirely, nor even of taking all the keys to the locks away from the executive organs of the state itself, but it does postulate that free access to information—including information of an official kind—is a supreme national good and that, as a general proposition, restrictions on publication in this field are more injurious to the nation than the damage which may be done by allowing such publication.

This conflict is by its nature incapable of resolution and it is not the business of this report to do more than state it and then describe how it is handled in a variety of countries. We begin at the libertarian end of the spectrum where the USA and Sweden provide the more illuminating examples. (Canada is considering a similar reform.)

USA

In the USA the libertarian strand, endemic in a country founded in revolt and nurtured at a distance from international conflicts, has had the exceptional boost of constitutional backing. The very first amendment to the Constitution, enacted in 1791, forbade the Congress of the United States to make any law "respecting an establishment of religion, or prohibiting the free exercise thereof; or of the press; or the right of the people peaceably to assemble, and to petition the Government for a redress of grievances." Thus in the USA freedom to publish has been the norm, at any rate in theory, and its abridgement has been seen as a derogation requiring positive justification whereas elsewhere in the world it has seemed normal to give governments the right to veil information and to require the proponents of disclosure to discharge the burden of justifying it.

Further, in 1966 Congress reinforced the libertarian generalisation by passing the Freedom of Information Act, which obliges all agencies of the federal government to make public their organization, procedures and policies and to make available to the public on request documents (excluding work-

30

ing papers) which do not fall into nine specifically reserved categories. In defence and foreign relations the government remains the arbiter of what shall or shall not be disclosed, but outside these areas the seeker after information may, if denied it, go to the courts for a ruling on the issue whether the documents in question do or do not come within the reserved categories. In adjudicating this issue the court will inform itself about the nature and contents of the documents and is not bound merely to accept the government's assertion that disclosure would be contrary to the national interest.

National security has not been thrown to the winds. One of the reserved categories comprises information excepted by statute and one pertinent statute is the Espionage Act which makes it a criminal offence to communicate information on national defence with reason to believe that this information could be used to harm the USA or, alternatively, to give advantage to a foreign state. (But the court does not in such a case have to infer that the information concerns national defence merely from the fact that it is classified. The government cannot shield itself from judicial scrutiny by putting a security tab on its documents.)

Procedurally as well as substantively the emphasis in the USA is libertarian rather than secretive. The Pentagon Papers case (*New York Times* vs. *United States*) is a well publicized example. In that case the government tried, on grounds of national security, to prevent the publication of official papers purloined from government custody. It failed owing to the pronounced reluctance of the courts, including the Supreme Court, to countenance any pre-trial restraint on publication, although it appears from the several judgments in the Supreme Court that the Court would do so if it were persuaded that publication would cause "direct, immediate and irreparable damage" to the nation. This phrase is an apt illustration of the weight of the burden which is imposed in the USA on any authority seeking to keep its documents from the public. The Pentagon Papers case, while it leaves open the possibility of proceedings against a publisher on other counts (e.g. theft), goes a long way to demolishing the obstacles to publishing in the first place. The Supreme Court gives a very high, although not absolute priority to the freedom to publish. It has done so partly no doubt in response to the profound, 200-year old American addiction to liberty but also—one may opine even more so—because the constitution itself contains provisions which can be invoked in aid of this freedom. The law, unusually, is on the side of disclosure.

Sweden

Sweden has no such ancient law but has enacted a modern one. It is the prime example of a country where the pendulum has swung decisively away from secrecy and in favour of publication. It has adopted the principle that official information not specifically labelled secret shall be available to the public and has formalized this principle in the Freedom of the Press Act (the benefits of which are not limited to the press). It expressly permits the publication of official papers by all and sundry, subject to exceptions of two kinds. Working papers are, as in the USA, not made available. The rationale is that decisions should be known but that the processes by which they are reached should not be exposed. Secondly, certain kinds of document, and the information in them, are embargoed for varying periods of time. These categories include defence and foreign affairs (50 years), cabinet papers (various periods), certain police and criminal records (up to 70 years), documents of the Bank of Sweden relating to the value of the currency and the level of reserves, and a variety of commercial, industrial, patent, judicial and parliamentary documentation. There are also provisions for the protection of individuals and their near relatives. Sweden, in effect, has been propelled by its liberal climate to try to define what shall be kept secret instead of allowing government to impose a general blanket of secrecy which publishers and the public probe at their peril.

But this approach is still exceptional. In most countries the dilemma between the right to know and the need to conceal is resolved by leaving in the hands of the state the right to decide what shall be concealed, a right which is most often vested in the state's executive organs. One consequence of giving the state unfettered or unsupervised discretion in these matters is to raise the suspicion outside government circles that the state abuses its discretion—in particular by classifying as secret material whose publication would not harm the nation but would embarrass the government. The dividing line between the threat to national security and mere executive inconvenience can be a blurred one, especially when seen from inside government.

Allied with official secrecy, properly so called, is the notion of confidentiality. This doctrine, long familiar and enforced in certain private relationships (e.g. lawyer and client, doctor and patient, confessor and penitent), has been extended to embrace information acquired in the course of public service by a Minister or civil servant.

France

French law is notably wide in these respects. Its prohibitions fall into two main categories: the defence of the nation and professional confidence. The former covers internal as well as external security and specifies four types of offender: the traitor who passes secret information to a foreign state; the foreign spy who does likewise; the functionary with official status or responsibilities who divulges such information, without however intending treason or espionage; and the person who does this but has no official responsibilities. Information in the second category, protected by reason of the confidential circumstances in which it is imparted, includes information given to some civil servants as well as to lawyers, doctors and priests. Receiving such information and giving it wider currency is not an offence unless the receiver played the part of an accomplice in the original disclosure or incited the civil servant, lawyer etc. to transgress his professional duty.

Great Britain

British law is even more stringent. The Official Secrets Act of 1911 (later amended by Acts of 1920 and 1939) was enacted in order to make life difficult for spies. It has done much more than that. It has been used to make life easier for Ministers and civil servants. To all intents and purposes any document or information generated by government is secret if the government chooses to say it is. It is a criminal offence for anybody in the service of the state, or having a contract with the state, to communicate to anybody else by words or by passing documents any information acquired in his official or contractual capacity. The wording of the prohibition is extremely wide. It is furthermore also a criminal offence for any person whatever to receive information of the kind described in the Act unless he can prove—and the burden of proof is on him—that he did so against his will.

The Act has become a means not merely to protect national security but also to conceal the processes of government. This situation has been increasingly attacked in recent years but no government has wished to change it. In 1971 a departmental committee (the Franks committee) was set up to consider one section of the Act. It reported (Cmd. 5104) in the following year, but its recommendations have been pigeon-holed and the obnoxiously wide provisions of the 1911 Act remain on the statute book. Changes in the law proposed by the new British government would do more harm than good.

In addition, the doctrine of confidentiality, which has been expanded by judicial interpretation during the present century, was invoked by government in an attempt to prevent publication of the diaries of the late Richard Crossman, who had been a cabinet Minister and member of the Privy Council. The attempt failed on somewhat narrow grounds and the British publisher will continue to steer clear of the multiple hazards of this branch of the law unless he is very angry or very rich. He will in consequence sometimes refrain from publishing even books which the law might not catch.

The only concession to free inquiry made in Britain in recent years has been the reduction from 50 years to 30 in the period for which official papers are normally withheld from public scrutiny. Since 1958 the general rule requires the transfer of all such papers after 30 years to the Public Record Office where they may be read and copied by any person of any nationality who procures the necessary pass (which presents no difficulties to bona fide researchers from serious scholars to the merely curious). But the government retains the right to make exceptions at its own discretion. These exceptions are sometimes, but not always, noted or otherwise evident. There is some disquiet about files which fail to reach the Public Record Office not because they have been deliberately held back on security grounds but because they have mysteriously disappeared in a less official manner, having been winnowed out of the mass of archivial material before this is sent on its way to the Public Record Office. An official committee is at present considering the custody of documents in government departments and the processes by which some are selected for the archives and others for the shredder.

None of this applies to documents under the "secret vote", that is to say, material which is the property of the secret intelligence services. This material is vouchsafed to the public only if and when the authorities decide *ad hoc* that it should be. There are in Britain no provisions governing the general release of such material and since, by definition, few people know what exists few agitate to see it. It is comparatively easier for government to preserve the cloak of secrecy over material of this special kind and nobody whatever is entitled to challenge the government's decision at law. No court has the right to question it.

The contrast between the extremes represented by United States legislation on the one hand and Britain's heavy-handed restrictiveness on the other was neatly illustrated in 1979 by the publication of the book *Sideshow* by William Shawcross, an exposure of the behaviour of Nixon and Kissinger over Cambodia. This book, by an Englishman, could not have been written if the subject matter had been British and not American. Shawcross would have been unable, in his own country, to get at the facts.

The defence of the state is commonly interpreted to include not only its defence against external enemies but also the maintenance of its internal stability and coherence. Part of a government's duty is to prevent the state from falling apart or being pulled apart either by a violent disruptive minority or by centrifugal forces which imperil the state as constituted. This situation arises most frequently in the new states whose statehood has not been confirmed by time, in states which have effected a social revolution which is not yet successfully secure, and in states composed of consciously distinct parts in competition or conflict with one another. Where the unity of the state is for any such reason fragile the constitution seeks to safeguard it with special provisions and the government is alert to defend it. Yugoslavia and Indonesia provide examples in this second category; West Germany in the first.

West Germany

In the 60's and 70's a number of countries experienced violent protest which, in the eyes of the authorities, bordered on revolution and was met by counter-violence and emergency measures, including censorship. The West German government toughened its criminal code by adding article 88a aimed against the anti-constitutional advocacy of criminal acts, against encouraging or supporting any act harmful to the existence or security of the federal republic, and against attacks on basic constitutional principles. The article expressly condemns the production, acquisition, circulation, stocking, offering, commending, importing and exporting of texts or parts of texts which fall within the article. The West German government resorted to censorship in order to prevent such groups as the Baader-Meinhof "gang" and the *Rote Armee Fraktion* (RAF) from stating their case and saying in books and pamphlets why they felt it right to kill people; to ban the description of revolutionary events in the past which might foster their re-enactment; and to forbid writers to quote proscribed views in such a way as to make these views their own.

Article 88a was enacted in January 1976. The climate which sanctioned this legislative toughness was made murkier in the following year by the hijacking of the Lufthansa airliner which was forced to land in Somalia, and by the kidnapping of the banker Hanns-Martin Schleyer and the assassination of the public prosecutor Siegfried Buback. But a number of disturbing cases affecting the freedom of publishing occurred even before these events.

One of the most disturbing concerned *Wie alles anfing* (*How It All Began*) by Bommi Baumann, an autobiographical account of how the author became an urban guerrilla, published by the firm of Trikont. The book was seized and banned. A separate edition of the same work was then published by 380 West Germans as a test case. It was not seized. The proprietors of Trikont, who had been brought to trial, were acquitted. Article 88a was then passed and the Trikont edition was again prosecuted, the prosecution alleging that all Trikont's publications were socialist works which were issued not to make money but to make political propaganda. The non-Trikont edition of the book, which remained unmolested, was distinguished on the grounds that it was a solitary venture. In effect therefore article 88a was being used not against a particular text but against a particular publisher.

Article 88a was also used against the book *Kampf gegen die Vernichtungshaft*, published in 1974 by the Kommittee gegen Folter an politischen Gefangenen in der BRD and successfully prosecuted in 1977. The book contained allegations of brutality and torture upon members of the Baader-Meinhof "gang". The truth of these allegations was not questioned at the trial but the author was sentenced to two years in prison on the grounds that, as a known political malcontent who had been engaged in violence, his resort to authorship was a continuation of his criminal activities by other means.

Die Herren des Morgengrauens by J. Chotjewiecz, an attack on police behaviour, was rejected by his usual publisher but accepted and published by another, the prominent left-wing Berlin house Rotbuch Verlag. He himself was prosecuted under article 88a for signing a resolution of protest against the conditions of incarceration of members of the RAF.

A history of German anarchists in Chicago, *Die deutschen Anarchisten in Chicago,* was seized by the Bavarian authorities because it explained how to make explosives and how to use them against the rich, the police and the army. The publisher, Wagenbach, appealed and won. (In Britain the writings of the Brazilian Communist Carlos Marighela, although published, were banned from a number of bookshops because they provided similar instruction.)

Again in 1977 a book first published in 1973 was not only banned in West Germany but also in a Danish library just within the West German state. This book—*Über den bewaffneten Kampf in Westeuropa*—was published by Verlag Rote Sonne in German in Utrecht and in the same year in Danish with the simplified title *Vaebnet Kamp.* It was banned in West Germany because it set out to make a case for the Baader-Meinhof "gang". A copy of the Danish edition was bought for the Danish library in Flensburg which is a town in Germany with a Danish population, Danish newspapers and schools and a Danish library staffed by Danes. (Similar situations in reverse exist on the other side of the German–Danish border.) The director of the Danish library was aware of a "black list" of forbidden books which West German libraries were not permitted to stock, but since neither the German local authorities nor the German library service had ever told him of the list's existence or contents he bought books freely in accordance with his own judgement and Danish practice. But in 1977 he was made aware by looking at the book's jacket that it was a banned book. Why he looked at the jacket at this point is not clear but, having done so, he withdrew it from stock. He denied that, in changing from Danish to German practice, he was influenced by censorship or self-censorship; he was acting, he said, in order to avoid a possible conflict with the law and because he regarded it as cheap and disloyal to stock a book which his West German colleagues were not allowed to stock. This incident reflects an unusual frontier situation, but by applying German practices in a Danish library on German soil the Danish librarian was, if unwillingly, drawing attention to the differences between the two countries. He was also giving rise to suspicions that the true reason for the withdrawal of the book was pressure from the German authorities.

Further evidence of such pressures has been provided by the librarian of Bremen University who was warned, by federal and Land authorities, that he risked prosecution if he were to issue on loan books published in German in Sweden about anarchist and "red" groups. This case was disclosed by Professor Ulrich Klug of Cologne University who is chairman of the recently established Committee for the Protection of Books—a private association of authors, publishers, printers and librarians created in 1979 to "combat... covert and overt prosecution, surveillance and hindrance of the publication of books and restrictions on the access to books...

Yugoslavia

Yugoslavia is another state where the government has felt justified in exercising extensive censorship in defence of the state itself. Created only 60 years ago, dismembered and occupied for 4 years during the Second World War, Yugoslavia is very much aware of its federal nature and the strains on its federal structure. Furthermore, its development during and after the war as a communist state with a difference has elevated its special brand of socialism to a sacrosanct status which its government is determined to entrench and defend against critical attack, including above all domestic criticism.

Article 118 of the Yugoslav criminal code sets out to protect the integrity of the state and its socialist philosophy in the following cumbrous terms:

"Whoever, by means of writing, speech or in any other way, advocates or in cites the violent or unconstitutional change of the social system or State organization, the overthrow of the representative agencies or their executive offices, the breakup of the brotherhood and the unity of the peoples of Yugoslavia, or resistance to decisions of representative agencies or their executive offices significant for the protection and development of socialist relationships, the security of the defence of the country; or whoever maliciously and untruthfully represents the social situation in the country shall be punished by strict imprisonment for not more than twelve years."

This article has been used to stifle the expression of Croat, Serb and other nationalisms whose resurgence might endanger public order or the very existence of the state. Freedom to publish in these areas is a fissiparous luxury—or so prevailing official mood has it. This is a classic case of ends and means. The object of promoting goodwill and preventing clashes between the peoples of Yugoslavia is indisputably an admirable one. The question is whether the means too are always acceptable.

Censorship has also been used against the political opponents of the regime even when these are not tainted by separatism. All the works, fiction as well as non-fiction, of Milovan Djilas are proscribed, including even his rendering of Milton's *Paradise Lost* and other translations. So are the books of Ljuba Tadic and other members of the so-called Praxis group (contributors to the marxist periodical *Praxis*) whose dissent from rigid orthodoxy in the late 60's and early 70's led to their dismissal from their professional posts at the University of Belgrade and to the suppression of *Praxis* itself by the expedient of ensuring that no printer would print it.

The government's specifically political concern is made the more manifest by the fact that many non-political but sensitive questions are fairly freely discussed in Yugoslavia, in books as well as in oral debate or conversation. They include moral issues such as sexual behaviour and drug-taking. What is kept under control is the national issue and particularly books on language or literature (including dictionaries) which might serve to heighten a separatist consciousness. (It was through language and literature that these and other European people asserted their individuality and their cultural and political rights against the Austrian and Turkish empires.) Tactics have varied. Some books have been prevented from appearing. Others have been banned after publication. Others have been allowed to appear and circulate but, as a result of official intervention, have had no reviews or only hostile ones.

Thus *Ognjište* (*The Hearth*) by Mile Budak, a tale of peasant life and a classic of Croat literature, is not allowed to be re-issued: the author, a former Minister of Education executed in 1946, was a prominent Croat nationalist who was on the losing side in the civil conflict which was fought during the Second World War. In 1971, at the time of the threatened explosion of Croat separatism, the entire edition of 40,000 copies of *The Croat Orthography,* about to be published by Skolska Knjiga of

Zagreb, was seized and (with a solitary exception which was smuggled out of the country) destroyed. In 1972 Vlado Gotovac, poet and former editor of the suppressed Croat weekly Hrvatski Tjednik, was sentenced to four years in prison and forbidden to publish any of his own works for four years after being charged with distorting the position of Croatia in the Yugoslav federation and propagating Croat separatism. Bans of this kind, which remain in force after a particular author has completed the sentence imposed upon him, appear to be unique to Yugoslavia, although they recall South Afircan legislation concerning "banned persons". References to the separate origins of the Croats, particularly to their allegedly non-Slav origins, are censored. On the other hand *Croat Literature and Language in the World Context,* published by Liber Publishing House, although sharply attacked, is allowed to circulate.

Among Serbs the popular novelist Dobrica Ćosić had one book—*Moc i Strepnje (Power and Foreboding)*—banned after publication on account of its "Greater Serbia" overtones. Ćosić has been stigmatized, with other writers, as having marked nationalist tendencies. But his other books, including his very successful tetralogy about Serbia in the First World War, circulate freely.

Recent history, where the presentation of the whole truth might appear to be an element of paramount importance, has been another subject for official interference. The role of Yugoslavia in the Second World War has been subject to censorship. The Slovene poet and Christian Socialist, Edvard Kocbek, a postwar Vice-President of the Slovene Republic, has had the greatest difficulty in getting his war diaries published more than 30 years after the events described in them; and although censorship has been relaxed in recent years, statistics about the number of persons killed during the war remain a closely guarded secret, locked away in the Institute of Military History in Belgrade. The history of the war is recognized as dangerous ground, so that writers wishing to do more than repeat the authorized version avoid the subject; it would be foolhardy to proceed without official sanction and it is believed that the necessary *imprimatur* would not be given in a dubious case without reference to Tito himself. The recent history of socialist Yugoslavia is a no-go area.

An extreme case of the censorship of information about the war occurred in 1974 when the writer Djuro Djurović was arrested ostensibly for merely reading *Tito, Mihailović and the Allies 1941–45* by Walter R. Roberts, an American book which gave a version of the activities of Tito's partisans which deviated from officially approved accounts. The case is a somewhat mysterious one, since the reading of whatever material is not an offence known to Yugoslav law. Djurović was a wartime adviser to Mihailović and the Četniks.

Another stretch of recent history which remains closed to writers is the prison camps on Goli Island. In the late 'sixties some attempts were made to write about these camps, which were established in 1948 and not closed until 1956, but in 1971 a play "When the Pumpkins were Blooming" was taken off after a short run in Belgrade. In the next year the novel *Levitan*, by the Slovene author Vitmil Zupan on his experiences in gaol on Goli, was set in type but then banned without explanation.

In at least one case the basis for this paternalism has been even wider and vaguer than concern for the unity of the Yugoslav nation. In 1972 the magazine *Gradina* was arraigned under a law forbidding the publication of material which falsely depicts self-management. The relevant issue of the magazine was banned for creating an incorrect interpretation of social conditions and so causing "anxiety among citizens".

Indonesia

A further example of the use of censorship in defence of the state is Indonesia. Here the law provides that books inspired by communism, marxism, or leninism have no right to appear. The Indonesian state is defined in terms of ideas as well as by geography. These ideas are five: the Panc Sila, i.e. belief in God, nationality, humanity, democracy and social justice. Anything considered hostile to these ideas is taboo. So are all the works of Sukharno and most books about him. Thus *Indonesia since Sukharno* by Peter Palomka, an Australian, was banned in 1972 and a major interview with Sukharno by Christianto Wibisono has been banned on the grounds that its publication would "disturb peace and order". This phrase was used too to prevent the publication in 1979 of a pamphlet entitled *Breaking the Shackles of Oppression*. This pamphlet was originally a plea for the defence in the trial of one of 36 students who were involved in demonstrations in June 1979 and were arrested and charged with the overlapping offences of disturbing peace and order and insulting the head of state. The ensuing trials took place in eight different states, in one of which the local authority banned the pamphlet. The ban was then made general by the federal authorities.

On the other hand, and notwithstanding the Panc Sila, a novel by A. K. Mihardja called *The Atheist,* has not been banned, and some publishers—notably Gunung Agung—succeed in publishing books which seem dangerously close to forbidden territory. It would seem that bargains may be struck. Gunung Agung's comparative freedom, for example, may have something to do with his withdrawal of a book on the inheritance of Sukharno after authorities had expressed their dislike of it.

India

Finally in this section we may notice the treatment in India of Colonel Saghal's book *The Unfought War* about the inglorious conduct of the war in the North East Frontier Agency. The book itself was not banned but pressures were used to prevent its serialization in an illustrated weekly and it is not a book which can easily be found inside military establishments.

Some modern states retain in their constitutions or general laws what are in effect attenuated vestiges of the old notion of *lèse-majesté*. That is to say, the state enjoys, as a legal person, some of the special protection that was once accorded to the monarch. This protection may also be extended to one or more of the higher dignitaries of the state, notably the President for the time being who, as the embodiment of the secular republic, has inherited some of the sacrosanctity of the anointed king: for example, satires directed against the present President of Portugal have been officially attacked and removed from circulation. But not only a President.

France

In France in 1969 Grasset was put under some pressure not to publish a book critical of Jacques Chaban-Delmas who was at that date Prime Minister. (M. Chaban-Delmas was not himself a party to this pressure.) There are, in other words, some whose respect for high office lead them to deplore attacks on the office-holder's behaviour on the grounds that such attacks assail the dignity of the state itself.

West Germany

The West German constitution makes it a special offence to disparage the republic, its Länder, symbols, anthem, president or constitutional organs. Defaming the president in his political capacity is more severely punishable than defaming him in his personal capacity, and no prosecution may be initiated in the former case without the president's consent. In a recent case in Baden-Württemberg an historical atlas was banned from use in schools on the footling grounds that, since the name BRD was not spelt out in full, the atlas was unsuitable for educational purposes.

Sweden

Sweden retains special, if somewhat meaningless, provisions protecting the members of its royal family and official personages.

Ireland

In Ireland it is specifically an offence to undermine the authority of the state—an exceedingly broad and vague threat.

Philippines

In the Philippines, with equal imprecision, it is an offence to advocate the overthrow of the established government. Provisions of this nature are not uncommon. Sometimes they are enshrined in a constitution or basic law, but they need not be so entrenched and have the same effect when enacted by normal legislative procedures. The only difference is that in the latter case they may be more easily altered.

Where official persons are protected in this way, the attacks which are punishable need not be physical attacks. They may be merely verbal and the essence of the offence is not so much false defamation as simple insult. Such personages are therefore being accorded wider legal privileges than the ordinary citizen or foreigner, who is not normally entitled to resort to the law unless what is said about him is untrue. But this view is not universal.

USA

In the USA public figures may have diminished rather than enhanced protection and may even be exposed without redress to false attacks for which their more private fellow citizens would be able to take legal action. This is because the freedom to criticize, buttressed by the First Amendment on the constitution, permits more searching attacks on those who have opted for the rewards and prominence of public office than on those who have chosen to remain private citizens.

The defence of the national interest may be extended to include favours for friendly governments and their officials and emissaries, and censorship of matters whose disclosure might impede the state's diplomacy and political aims.

West Germany – France

Privileges and immunities for diplomats have been part of the current coin of international intercourse since the origins of permanent diplomatic missions at the time of the European Renaissance, but in modern times these courtesies have been extended by special annexes to the criminal law. In West Germany, for example, it is an offence under the constitution to insult heads or other representatives of foreign states when they are officially upon the territory of the Federal Republic— provided however that the foreign state in question accords the same privileges to West Germany's president and emissaries. In France it is an offence to insult not only a foreign head of state but also Ministers of External Affairs and Ambassadors. Furthermore, foreign heads of state are entitled under French law to ask the French government to seize a book which gives them offence. Whether, given the existence of laws of this kind, the government will take action in a particular case depends in the main on actual political circumstances, i.e. on essentially unpredictable concatenations of events. Governments like to have the power to act, even though they may as a rule prefer to refrain. In 1978, when Editions du Seuil were about to publish *La Sentinelle de Staline,* a book giving an unflattering picture of Enver Hoxha's Albania, the Albanian embassy in Paris pressed the publishers not to publish but the French government remained deaf to pleas to intervene directly in order to prevent abuse of a country with which France was maintaining correct diplomatic relations. Presumably the French government, weighing one thing against another, concluded that the game was not worth the candle.

But circumstances alter cases. Two years earlier the government decided the other way when, in October 1976, the entire edition of *Prison d'Afrique* by Jean-Paul Alata was seized as it was being despatched from the printer to Seuil. The seizure was effected under the very law of 1881 which proclaims the freedom of publishing.

Prison d'Afrique described conditions in Guinean prison

camps. Its suppression had nothing to do with the truth or falsity of anything in the book. It was seized by the Ministry of the Interior at the prompting of the Ministry of Foreign Affairs because its publication was presumed to be injurious to current attempts to improve Franco-Guinean relations, i.e. for *raisons d'état*. It was not seized in pursuance of a request by Sekou Touré as a foreign head of state; the Guinean President made, so far as is known, no such request. The government used a clause in the law of 1881 which gave the Minister of the Interior authority to ban books of foreign origin (*de provenance étrangère*). *Prison d'Afrique* was written in French, in France and by a Frenchman and it was to be published by a French publishing house, but because Alata had been deprived of his nationality in 1958 at the time of the breach between France and Guinea, the Minister decided that he was a foreigner and his book therefore *de provenance étrangère*. All of which goes to show not only what repressive use may be made of a law passed to guarantee the freedom to publish, but also how far the concept of national security may be stretched—in this case to embrace the assumed susceptibilities of a foreign state and to place them above the freedom to publish the truth. Finally, since the book was suppressed by Ministerial decree and not by judicial process (the courts had declared that they had no competence in the matter) the publisher had no right of appeal.

USSR

Diplomatic considerations may take subtler forms. Finnish publishers have to exercise a discreet self-censorship over what they publish about the USSR; they would be mad not to. Even in more distant Yugoslavia, fifteen years after the breach with the USSR, Mihajl Mihajlov was sentenced to nine months in prison for his criticism of the USSR in his book *Moscow Summer*. Solzhenytsin's *Gulag Archipelago* has not appeared in Yugoslavia, although Karlo Stejner's *7 000 Days in Siberia* has been not only published (1972) but reprinted. Solzhenytsin's other works have been published in Yugoslavia but the publication of *Gulag* is presumably considered too great an affront.

Finland

Nor has *Gulag* found a publisher in Finland, where publishers have to tread delicately for obvious politico-geographical reasons.

There was a time when state and church were so intimately associated that the powers of the state were more or less automatically deployed in defence of religion or of a particular creed or established church. Writers and publishers were not free to say what they pleased about these things. This is now rarely the case. Formally established religions exist in countries as diverse as Denmark, England, Finland, Italy, Norway, Sweden, Spain, Venezuela and the Swiss canton of Ticino. But in all these places, including those with an established church, there is in law freedom to criticize it, to question its tenets and to promote a rival religion. Switzerland constitutes a partial anomaly since in Switzerland the cantons and not the federal government have the jurisdiction to establish a particular religion or sect and to ban proselytizing.

Many countries have laws against blasphemy. In law blasphemy is a special form of libel. It is widely, although by no means universally, regarded as anachronistic. As a result anti-

51

blasphemy laws are not much used, even where they remain unrepealed. Norway's anti-blasphemy law was last invoked in 1930. In Ireland there has been no prosecution since 1922. In Denmark the law against insulting any religious community's teaching or practices was invoked in the 1930's to protect Jews against Danish Nazis but has since fallen into desuetude. In England, however, after half a century without a prosecution, a private prosecutor recently brought proceedings against the magazine for homosexuals, *Gay News*. The case went all the way to the House of Lords where in 1979 the House decided, by the narrowest majority, that the offence of blasphemy is committed when the accused can be shown to have intended to publish material which, in the opinion of a jury, is likely to shock or cause resentment. This judgement means that the prosecutor does not have to show that the accused intended to shock or cause resentment; the only intention to be proved against the accused is the intention to publish.

Blasphemy in English law applies only to the Christian religion. One may be as offensive as one wishes about other religions and their gods without committing blasphemy (although other offences may be committed). Similarly, Spain prohibits insults to the beliefs, rites and ceremonies of Roman Catholics only. It is unlikely that discrimination of this kind is confined to these two countries.

3. The Defence of Morals

The second general area where the state claims to have a special duty is the defence of morals and good behaviour. The office of censor was instituted in Europe when the patriarchal patricians of the ancient Roman republic endowed public officials with a replica of their executive authority over domestic behaviour. Nowadays the supervision of morals means above all sexual morals. The state, with at least some and often much popular assent, is the principal agent in regulating indecency, obscenity and pornography.

Denmark

The *locus classicus* on pornography is Denmark where in 1967 restrictions on the production and distribution of "obscene publications" were removed by parliament. Two years later similar restrictions on obscene pictures and objects were also removed, except in relation to their display and sale to persons under 16 years of age.

The immediate cause of this action was a decision in 1964 by the Supreme Court which refused to condemn a Danish language edition of John Cleland's *Fanny Hill* (notwithstanding that the original English edition had earlier been banned).

There were also more general reasons. Denmark had already become a centre for the production, dissemination and export of vast quantities of pornography, both in fiction and in the form coyly described as sex education. According to sampling surveys made in the 'sixties this kind of literature had become familiar to something like three-quarters of the adult female population and a much higher proportion of males. This avidity both betokened a change in the moral climate and gave an air of unreality to laws designed to prevent its gratification. These laws were not only, as is the nature of laws seeking to define obscenity, so imprecise as to lead to conflicting court judgements; they were also out of tune with current social attitudes. To liberals who believe that law should reflect society's wishes the laws had lost their validity. Even conservatives, more apt to stress the regulative function of laws, joined in supporting the experiment of doing away with them: Denmark had a conservative government in these years. Psychologists were able to point out that the appetite for pornography was easily sated, as the demand for books of this kind rapidly fell within two years of their becoming freely available. The demand which had preceded and conduced to liberalization turned out to be evanescent, although pornographic magazines continued to flourish after the afflatus had gone out of the book trade.

But even in Denmark there are limits, as the following recent case of legally backed censorship shows. The case concerned children. In the small market town of Thisted in West Jutland the mayor and town council refused in 1977 to allow a local library to stock two children's books, *Katamaran* and *Sabotage* by Bengt Haller. The mayor, who admitted that he had not read the books, accepted from his colleagues on the council the view that Haller's language was offensively "basic". The mayor also objected to the payment of a fee to Haller for a talk given by him in the public library. The mayor was in effect claiming control by the council over the use of public funds—while in so far as his objections related to the purchase of books, the library's committee joined issue with him on the grounds that it was wrong for the council to use its control over the library's budget to veto the purchase of particular books. Some members of the council supported the library committee, partly because they disapproved of censorship and partly on the practical grounds that, if the mayor were right, every change in the composition of the council could lead to a purge of the library's shelves. The town's cultural committee sided with the mayor. The acting librarian resigned. The affair assumed national proportions. The Minister of Culture criticized the mayor and council for interfering in matters which they did not understand and in contravention of the rules of the library service. The issue went to litigation and in May 1979 the court ruled that the mayor and council had acted *intra vires*.

Finland – The Netherlands – Sweden

Denmark's almost, but not completely, untrammelled freedom of publication is approached in Finland, The Netherlands and Sweden but most countries shrink from so much freedom where morality can be invoked. Since the alternative to freedom is to define and forbid, the practical issue is how to define what shall be forbidden. The generally prevailing rule is to permit criticism of traditional patterns of behaviour and traditional taboos, to allow writers to propagate unconventional views and even unconventional behaviour, but to interfere more heavily where sex comes in and particularly where children may be involved. The problem of definition becomes therefore the problem of defining pornography or obscenity, a matter which the law finds peculiarly difficult.

For the most part criminal codes forbid obscenity without saying at all clearly what it is. It is taken to be self-evident, and there is without question a mass of published material which is evidently indecent or obscene in the eyes of anybody willing to admit that indecency and obscenity exist. Problems arise in relation to two questions: whether indecency and obscenity should be banned (the Danish argument already discussed); and, if some censorship is to be imposed, how to adjudicate the borderline case. In countries where codes or statutes may be supplemented by reference to judicial decisions in particular cases, some guidance may be obtained by studying these past decisions; but definitions cannot be relied upon to stay the same since they can be defined only by reference to shifting criteria.

USA

In the USA, for example, the principal touchstones of obscenity are two: local community standards (which necessarily differ from area to area) and the worthlessness of the publication. To be obscene a publication must, as a whole, lack literary, artistic, political and scientific value (as to which opinions necessarily differ but evidence may be given).

France

The French penal code forbids "l'outrage aux bonnes mœurs", thus leaving the field wide open. The courts have attempted to make the law more specific and have defined pornography as anything which depraves "les bonnes mœurs" by removing the emotional content from the rites of love or by describing only its physiological mechanism, if in so doing "deviations are encouraged with obvious relish". Deviancy becomes therefore the touchstone of pornography, but whether this description is much help, or whether it is the only one, are questions without clear answers.

The unsatisfactoriness of legislation in these fields is further underlined by the fact that a law introduced in France in the 30's to keep out Nazi propaganda is being used forty years later to keep out Swedish pornography. The state uses an old and essentially irrelevant weapon instead of seeking specific legislative authority to achieve its ends.

Great Britain

The English experience and a recent attempt to deal with it exemplify the problem. For over a century the central issue in a prosecution for obscene publication was the accused's intention to deprave or corrupt. This led to some notable bans, including D. H. Lawrence's *The Rainbow* and translations of Zola, Flaubert and Maupassant. In 1959 a new statute permitted an accused to plead that the work had literary, artistic or scientific merit or was otherwise of benefit to the public. This was an attempt to define obscenity by reference to the content of the book in addition to its presumed corrupting effects. It set up a new conflict between corruption on the one hand and literary etc. value on the other and left the jury with the (non-factual and subjective) role of saying how valuable an obscene book had to be in order to escape condemnation, or how obscene a valuable book had to be in order to earn it. It tried to define parameters in response to a feeling that the philistines and moralizers had been having rather too much of the argument.

In practice therefore, and given the inevitable limits to all attempts to define obscenity with any precision, what counts is the attitude of the authorities who will themselves be reacting in some measure to changes in the intellectual climate and also to pressure groups resisting or promoting such changes.

Israel

In Israel, for example, the presence of religious parties in coalition governments acts as a brake on permissiveness, ensures the maintenance of laws against the distribution of pornography—and drives it underground without much reducing the amount available to those who know where to ask for it.

Philippines

The experience of the Philippines shows how unpredictable the ebb and flow of official interference can be. Before and immediately after the Second World War there was a spate of book-burning at the instigation of the (Roman Catholic) Holy Name Society, but this activity has—at least temporarily —declined. The most objectionable, because the most arbitrary, official actions are those of authorities empowered to seize and confiscate without judicial fiat. The commonest cases arise at frontiers where customs officers have the power to seize and destroy. The argument in favour of such powers is that they expeditiously and economically stop the flow of indubitably disgusting material.

Ireland

But some right of appeal to a court is a needful check on such powers and some guarantee of expedition: in 1976, to cite a particularly outrageous example, the Irish customs seized a copy of *Jaws,* which had already sold 100,000 copies in Ireland, and referred it to the Censorship Board which eventually cleared it for distribution but only after a delay of nine months. Publishers live in dread of the wayward actions of the untutored customs officer.

The most straightforward example of censorship in defence of morality is provided by Ireland. The constitution of 1937 itself (article 40) limits the right of the citizen to the free expression of his "convictions and opinions", for the constitutional guarantee of this freedom is immediately cut back by these words: "The education of public opinion being, however, a matter of such grave import to the common good, the State shall endeavour to ensure that organs of public opinion, such as the radio, the press, the cinema, while preserving their rightful liberty of expression, including criticism of Government policy, shall not be used to undermine public order or morality or the authority of the State. The publication or utterance of blasphemous, seditious, or indecent matter is an offence which shall be punishable in accordance with law".

This limitation has been implemented by a number of statutes, some of which were passed during the English ascendancy (which was, however, relatively liberal in these matters) and so before the creation of the present Irish state—e.g. the Customs Consolidation Act of 1876. With the creation of the independent Irish state censorship found favour with booksellers because most books in circulation were published outside the jurisdiction with the consequence that the publishers and authors could not be prosecuted and the bookseller found himself in the front line. Censorship then flourished until the growth of radio and television introduced media which are inherently more difficult to police. In recent years censorship has been tempered by a combination of a changing climate of opinion, technological innovation and a certain retreat by the Roman Catholic Church from its dominance in secular affairs.

At present the principal relevant statutes are the Censorship Acts of 1929, 1946 and 1967. The effect of the most recent of these, together with a judgement of the High Court in 1978, is to restrict the rigours of censorship.

Censorship is exercised by a Board of Censors which has five members, appointed by the Minister of Justice. The Board considers books and periodicals sent to it by any person or by customs officers, whose duty includes searching for offensive material and who in fact provide the Board with about four fifths of what it reviews. The Board may also examine books (but seemingly not periodical publications) on its own initiative. It is provided by statute with no definition of indecency or obscenity. It is obliged by the 1947 Act to take into consideration the book's literary, artistic, scientific or historic merit; its language; and the nature and extent of the circulation, and class of reader, which the Board thinks it will have. A ban requires at least three affirmative votes and may not be imposed if two members of the Board vote against it, i.e. a minority may prevail on the side of publication provided it is not a minority of one. There is a right of appeal to a five-man Appeals Board.

Until 1967 a ban by the Censorship Board endured indefinitely. The Act of that year provides that every ban for indecency or obscenity shall be for 12 years only. It may be reimposed by the Board for further periods of 12 years.

In addition to banning books as indecent or obscene the Board is empowered to prohibit the sale and distribution of books which advocate contraception by unnatural means, the procurement of abortion or miscarriage, or any treatment or appliance conducive to these practices. The 12-year rule does not apply to this category. Under the Health Family Planning Act, which is expected to come into force this year (1979), the ban on the advocacy of unnatural contraception will be removed from the scope of the Board.

A register of prohibited publications is published officially. The 12-year rule has substantially reduced this list which used to extend from Ovid (in English), through the Kama Sutra and Sir Richard Burton's translation of the Thousand and One Nights, to a more or less predictable clutch of twentieth century celebrities, many of whom would be all but universally deemed to show high literary merit.

No priest has ever been a member of either Board, there is no automatic link between the Board's bans and the Vatican's Index of Prohibited Books, and the business of censorship has been passing increasingly from the purview of the Church to that of the elected legislature. In particular the Church, while continuing to censure most forms of contraception, has accepted that the law must be made by parliament. In the 1930's the secular authorities barred a book which had received the *imprimatur* of the archdiocese of Westminster.

Until very recently the Board and Appeals Board have operated independently of the Courts. Appeals were rare, mainly because the principal victims (British publishers) felt that it was not worth the time, trouble and money which an appeal entailed. Since 1978, however, and as a result of judicial decision, the rulings of the Board have become subject to review by the Courts which have established their right to overrule the Board—and to make the Board or its (unpaid) members bear the costs of such proceedings. This outcome has caused some surprise and confusion and it is not clear how the Minister of Justice, who has been asked by the Board to make new regulations, will resolve it. It arose this way.

The Board banned as "indecent or obscene" a booklet on family planning issued by the Irish Family Planning Association. The publishers appealed to the High Court which granted a conditional order directing the Board to show cause why its order should not be quashed on the grounds that the Board failed to give the author and publisher the opportunity to defend themselves. The Board replied that the Act of 1946 authorized but did not require it to communicate with author and publisher, and that this practice had never been regarded as mandatory. In upholding the appeal in July 1978 the Court ruled that the ban had been "against natural justice". But instead of remitting the case to the Board for further and more proper consideration the Court went on to rule on the substance of the case in issue and condemned the ban on the grounds that the Family Planning Association was conducted by responsible and qualified persons and that the booklet, so far from being pornographic or lewdly commercial, aimed simply to give basic factual information "on a delicate topic as to which there is genuine concern". Thus the Court, while not pronouncing upon the constitutionality of censorship as such, both criticized the Board's routine practices and asserted the Court's inherent authority to review and overturn the Board's decisions. The Board was told that it was required to give notice of a ban and allow submissions unless the defendants could not be found or the publication was "manifestly indecent or obscene". A judgement of this nature should be seen as something more than an interpretation of statute law. It is also an indication of a changing climate of opinion about the proper limits of censorship.

The curious position of Trinity College in Dublin deserves a passing reference. The College's library is a copyright library which, together with four others in the British Isles, receives under British law a copy of every book published in the United Kingdom. These books are normally despatched to the favoured libraries by the publisher before publication and so reach the library before there is any question of their being banned by the Irish censors. If and when one of them is banned the librarian removes it and its card reference and puts it in a special cupboard. The government allows the library to keep the book, since it has been acquired by statutory dispensation, but the library may not display it. It may, however, be produced for a reader upon written request to the librarian. An equally bizarre rule prevails in public libraries. Banned books may not be destroyed since they have been bought with taxpayer's money (books may be burned but not money); they have to be removed from the shelves, wrapped in brown paper and sealed. From time to time the Ministry of Justice sends officials to see whether the seals have been broken.

New Zealand

In New Zealand the Indecent Publications 1963 established the Indecent Publications Tribunal which works in much the same way as its Irish counterpart. It earned a reputation for liberality by classifying as not indecent the *Little Red School Book*, which, first published in Danish, was banned in Britain when translated into English.

4. The Civil Law

The publisher may be hampered by the civil law as well as the criminal law. The civil law is concerned neither to protect national security nor to uphold standards of behaviour but to safeguard the right and reputations of the individual.

Thus the law protects copyright and in so doing prevents or limits the republication of copyright material. This is not in general a matter for complaint and it is one of the comparatively few areas of the law which can show a significant degree of international accord and regulation. There are diverse views about how far the letter of the law ought to be relaxed, by legislation or convention, in order to permit verbatim quotation of copyright material in textbooks or other educational or scholarly works; and there are major issues on copyright arising out of modern technology and out of the needs of poverty-stricken countries. But with these matters this report has nothing to do.

The impact of the civil law on the freedom to publish can virtually be summed up in the one word: libel. Libel laws are a serious and constant hazard for the publisher in certain countries where, to the publisher at any rate, they appear unduly strict. While these laws vary greatly from country to country the general principle is uniform. The law of libel protects the individual against statements which harm his repute or standing and are in addition false. The publisher's problems arise in many ways.

First, in publishing a defamatory statement made by an author the publisher may not know that it is false. Yet he may be, and nearly everywhere is, no less answerable to the defamed person, even if he has taken reasonable steps to inquire into the truth of the false statement.

Secondly, he may be virtually certain that the statement is true but be unable to prove it, or uncertain of his ability to prove it to the satisfaction of a judge or jury. Since the burden of proof will be on him in an action at law, he will hesitate to publish and probably decide not to. If the subject matter is one of public interest he will feel that he has been prevented from performing a public service and he may well be right.

Thirdly, the publisher suffers a special disadvantage where a plaintiff succeeds in getting an interim injunction, or pre-trial restraint order, which obliges him to suspend publication pending the trial of the action. The trial may not come on for months, in which case the order has the effect of stopping publication before trial as if the trial had taken place and the publisher had lost. As every publisher knows, it is not easy to get a suspended book moving again, so that even if he is vindicated at the trial, the book may have been effectively killed.

Thus the law of libel, and particularly the incidence of pre-trial proceedings, operate to dissuade a publisher not merely from uttering libels but also from publishing truths which could be made the subject of actions for no purpose other than to suppress the truth. A plaintiff may use the law not in order to get damages for injury to his character, but in order to prevent by threats the exposure of his character.

The countries where complaint is loudest on this score are Britain and Ireland and, generally speaking, the problem of libel is acuter for publishers in these countries—and in other countries which have inherited English law and procedures—

than elsewhere. In England disquiet led to the appointment in 1971 of an official committee "to consider whether, in the light of the working of the Defamation Act 1952, any changes are desirable in the law, practice and procedure relating to actions of defamation". The committee (the Faulks Committee) reported in 1975. It found that changes were desirable. To date no changes have been made. Not the least remarkable thing about the report (Cmd. 5909) is the way governments have felt able to ignore it.

The report, with appendices and dissentient comments, is a long one. It includes a draft Bill to replace the 1952 Act and amend nearly a dozen other Acts. The general tenor of the report and the draft Bill is to relax the law in certain respects in favour of a defendant. Of particular interest to publishers is a proposal which, in the summary of recommendations at the end of the report, is headed "Special Protection for Book Publishers and Authors" and which reads as follows:

> "Where a plaintiff has either expressly or implicitly requested a defendant to withhold, withdraw or correct a book he should not be entitled to recover additional damages on the ground that a defendant continued to publish or failed to correct the book as requested, unless the plaintiff has given an undertaking to compensate that defendant for any loss incurred by him in complying with the request if the action should fail or be struck out."

Other proposed changes of particular interest include changes in the use of the terms "fair comment" and "malice". Much of the complaint directed against the law of libel has come from newpaper and periodical publishers rather than book publishers, but the latter have increasing reason to be concerned about libel laws in countries where the superfluity of journalists leads many of them to put out more of their work in book form. And everywhere obstacles of this nature are made the more fiercesome by the costs of defending an action in the courts.

The law on contempt of court also inhibits publishers. Here too Britain stands out as the place where the topic has been accorded serious and official attention—followed by inaction.

Again in 1971 an official committee (the Phillimore Committee) was established to consider whether any changes were required in the law. It reported in 1974 (Cmd. 5794), recommending modest changes. It found that uncertainties in the law were curbing freedom of expression and proposed the creation by statute of new defences in contempt cases. The root of the problem, so far as the publisher is concerned, is the conflict between the freedom to publish and inform the public on the one hand and, on the other, the right of a litigant or accused person to a fair trial: the publication may prejudice the right. The law on contempt in English law and in legal systems derived from it has been made to appear unduly strict by the proliferation of the popular press which, over the past century and more, has—with a fair measure of popular assent—arrogated to itself the functions of watchdog and detective but finds itself frustrated in the performance of these public duties. The recommendations of the Phillimore Committee, which apply to book publishers as well as journalists, go some way towards recognizing and alleviating these disabilities by proposing, first, that responsible discussion of matters at issue in civil proceedings should be free up to the opening of the trial of an action and, secondly, that comment during trial should be restricted only so far as publication might impinge on evidence likely to be given in the absence of the jury.

The restrictiveness of English law has also been recently

exposed in the so-called thalidomide case in which the *Sunday Times* carried its appeals against the muzzling of comment to the European Court of Human Rights. These proceedings concerned the permissible limits on the discussion of the merits of a case in the civil courts, particularly where the publication of facts or comment could be construed as pressure influencing the jury's assessment of damages. Whereas the English legal system concentrates in the first place on the administration of justice and the assurance of a fair trial, the European Court gives an equivalent or higher emphasis to freedom of speech. The effect of the European approach as opposed to the English is materially to shift the onus on prosecution and defence, since the former tolerates only such restrictions on comment as can be justified in a particular case as being necessary for a fair trial.

5. State Competition, Patronage and Taxation

Traditionally the state has interfered with the publisher's business by prohibiting the publication of certain facts or opinions. Increasingly, however, publishers find that they need to pay attention to the state not so much because of what it bans but because of what it does. The state is itself a publisher, in competition with other publishers and sometimes on preferential terms. The state also affects the sales of books either by buying them in significant quantities or by recommending or not recommending them—particularly in the educational sector.

The scale of these activities by the state has increased, is increasing and ought in the view of many publishers to be diminished or contained.

As a publisher the state has long been the source of official papers, government reports, museum catalogues, maps and charts and other offshoots of the business of governing. But it frequently ventures much further. In Britain, to take a pronounced example, Her Majesty's Stationery Office is not only the largest publishing enterprise in the country but has a range of publications which embraces practically everything except contemporary fiction and rubbish. Its books normally appear at prices comparable with those of commercial publishers, although it recently published at £10 a 600-page book which a commercial publisher would have issued at nearly double that price—a subsidy which the non-book-buying taxpayer might well not approve. In the Netherlands competition from official publications is described as "not yet" a threat, in Japan and Venezuela more succinctly as no threat. In Italy it is recognized as competition but not as a threat. Sweden reports that there is much state publishing but that it cannot be called unfair.

French, Bolivian and Indonesian publishers on the other hand describe state and state-financed publishing as incontestably a threat, and the West Germans agree. They say that state publishing is increasing and unfair and that commercial publishers are fighting a losing battle against its encroachments. The Norwegian judgement is the most discriminating. Public documents, say the Norwegians, should be published by the state and in any case nobody else wants to publish them; the literature of scientific research has also passed largely away from the traditional general publishers; but text-book publishing for schools is something that these publishers want to retain, arguing that a state text-book house is a menace to the variety of a publisher's list and so to its viability.

The conflict between private and public enterprise is focussed for the time being principally on books for schools. From the Indians and the Swiss, who state baldly that state publishing in education is a menace, through others who express their apprehensions less urgently, there is general agreement that the invasion of educational publishing by the state menaces publishing in general by depriving it of profit. The existing state of affairs is something of a compromise. State publishing flourishes in many countries but without attaining monopolistic proportions. The state is even wary of capturing too much of the market. In Sweden, for example, where the state textbook house has about 25 % of the market, it has said that it does not want more. And its commercial rivals concede that in seeking adoptions or recommendations it operates without special favours.

Publishing by broadcasting authorities provokes similar cries of unfair competition. In Britain the BBC has considerably enlarged its publishing in recent years and, to the chagrin of other publishers, has taken to publishing best-sellers based on successful television series (e.g. Kenneth Clark on Civilization and Alistair Cooke on America). The incomparable—and free—publicity provided by the television series which give birth to these publications enhances the sense of unfairness among British publishers who hate to see these books removed from their purview. They complain that the BBC has joined the publishing world on unfair terms. They would like to see something closer to the model obtaining in Sweden where publishing of this kind has declined and now consists predominantly of series linked with educational broadcasts. On the whole, publishers see unfair competition by broadcasting authorities as a potential rather than an actual threat.

Direct competition by the state and public authorities in the book trade and in schools is not the only aspect of official intervention in publishing. The state and its organs may be purchasers of books on a big scale or, as patrons, agents which determine how many books are bought by others. Public libraries and schools are affected in this way.

Library sales provide a sizeable part of a publisher's revenue, and where libraries are substantially dependent on government funds fluctuations in government spending seriously affect publisher's fortunes. Thus, in recent months cutbacks in public spending in the USA have reduced the buying of one public library system (El Paso) by half and another (New Orleans) by two thirds. In California the economy drive embodied in Proposition 13 put a stop to library extensions in the state,

71

and reports from many parts of the country describe the resentment of publishers and others when they discover that libraries are suffering larger cuts in their allocations than police, fire-fighting and other public services. The current cutting of public expenditure in Britain has had clear repercussions on British publishers. Even where economies, and the priorities observed in effecting them, seem reasonable or unavoidable, they are also facts which, when they make their unwelcome appearance, underline the extent of publisher's dependence on government policies. Where governments give, they have the power to stop giving. And they often do so with little or no notice.

In schools the state or its subordinate organs may be the principal purchaser of classroom books, although the choice of books for the school or class library is often freer. There is a spectrum of more or less delicately adjusted supervision. For example: in West Germany primary and secondary textbooks are licensed by the authorities which, without advancing a point of view of their own, try to ensure a balance. In Sweden and in Venezuela the equivalent authorities make or withhold recommendations and so indirectly influence choices without imposing them. In Norway the authorities pronounce upon the pedagogical adequacy of a book, thus in effect exercising a veto on professional grounds; they are not accused of abusing this power and would presumably be restrained from doing so by the climate of opinion and a free press. In Indonesia the state influences buying patterns in similar ways. In Ireland there is a list of "sanctioned" books for primary (but not secondary) schools; books are submitted in advance for official approval on pedagogical grounds, and the withholding of this approval—sometimes for trivial reasons—is a serious clog on its sales. In India the government recently refused to approve two history books but did not prohibit their use; there have been numerous complaints from Indian authors of decisive official discouragement, particularly of books on history or politics which displease somebody in authority. In Israel teachers who want to be in the good books of the Ministry of Education's inspectors (who may themselves be authors of relevant books) pay special attention to their recommendations. India reports similar temptations on teachers to buy what they know will be approved, and there must be many other places where caution or servility plays this role. Most teachers do not want to waste time doing battle with local school governors or boards.

The publisher is influenced in his turn. Confronted with a new educational manuscript, he will ask himself not merely how good it is but also whether it will find favour with those whose favours count. This is not merely a nuisance. It can also be corrupting. Those who need favours seek them. The means may be anything from the unexceptionable to the disgraceful. The publisher may seek out an author for no better reason than that he can get his book prescribed by his friends in authority or even, in an extreme case, by himself; the authorship of the book becomes more important than its contents, the title page more important than the rest of it. Where a prescription can make or break a book the publisher feels bound, in his author's interest as well as his own, to solicit favours by means ranging from persuasive talk to the over-generous hospitality which has become conventional in competitive business enterprises. Competition fosters many virtues but competition for contracts or sales does not promote integrity.

Control over the choice of books for school classrooms and school libraries is a specially delicate matter. The reasons are obvious. The argument that the immature child needs protection commands wide support—even though there is plenty of room for further argument about where immaturity ends and maturity begins, and about the dangers of retarding maturity by too much cosseting of the allegedly immature. The child is a special case, the school is where most children can best be conditioned by persons other than their parents, and the case for "catching them young" (with whatever purpose) is one of the commonplaces of social and intellectual history.

Controversy arises in two main areas. The one is political and impugns motives. The other is ethical and impugns good sense. In the one case critics allege that those who seek to ban certain books have a concealed or half concealed political motive. The commonest cases in the western world concern the exclusion of left wing material by right wing authorities or groups which do not want the children to grow up with left wing ideas. What such groups regard as left wing may vary very greatly indeed. The same can be just as true in reverse and to the discredit of left wing authorities, while in the communist dictatorships rigorous intervention by the authorities ensures that children get only a caricature of right wing views and none at all of liberal ideas.

The second case runs the gamut from attempts to shield children from unsavoury violence, through attempts to delay their acquaintance with sex, to positive measures—believed by their champions to be morally or religiously imperative—to stop the teaching of specified facts or theories.

Where does the publisher stand in all this? He is involved materially as the producer of a book which has been banned or as the intending publisher of a book which he has reason to fear will be banned. His publishing is therefore impeded. He is also involved to the extent—which, in education publishing, is not inconsiderable—that he is part of the cultural scene.

The direct intervention of government on political or ideological grounds is now endemic and it would be simpler to cite countries where it has not occurred than those where it has. Examples have been given in chapter 1 but the particular case of interference in education has been reserved to the present chapter.

A characteristic example is provided by Argentina where, after the military coup of 1976, orders were issued to comb libraries in secondary schools and institutions of higher education and remove "undesirable" books. The context of this action was unmistakably political and the definition of the offending material typically vague. Apologists, who include some Argentinian publishers, regard this kind of censorship as right and proper and describe it as a necessary redressing of the errors of teachers who have abused their freedom by using the wrong books in the past. Piaget and Freud are among authors regarded as undesirable in schools and colleges. Among children's books banned is *La Anti-Bomba,* a story about people who try to prevent their ruler from making war on a neighbouring country merely because he wants to, and force him to abandon the war and stop making bombs. This story has been declared to be "pernicious" and the publishers were consigned to prison for several months. In 1977 the same publishers, Daniel and Maria Ana Divinsky, owners of Ediciones de la Flor, were arrested for appealing against a ban on another children's book, *Cinco Dedos,* a translation of a West German publication. The Minister of Education has the power to ban any book which is specifically designed for educational use.

Behaviour of this kind is a normal concomitant of a coup, e.g. in Greece after 1967. More recently, in 1975, the Uruguayan government embarked upon a post-coup purge of politically unacceptable books from secondary schools, in the course of which 20,000 books in the Department of Education's own library were destroyed and two lists were circulated to schools—a list of definitely offensive books and a second list of books suspected of being subversive. These bans covered not only the social sciences—their main target—but also the natural sciences and languages which, in the opinion of the Department's Director of Secondary Education, could "introduce concepts damaging to the co-ordination of classical western thought". Two years later, in 1977, a further list was issued of books to be banned from primary schools; the authors include Antonio Machado, Pablo Neruda, Miguel Angel Asturias, Rafael Alberti and Nicolas Guillén as well as well known Uruguayan writers of children's fiction.

Local authorities, acting *proprio motu* or at the instigation of local groups, are as prone as central governments to intervene in the selection of school books. A number of member Associations report that, in their countries, books are never—or hardly ever—banned from classrooms or school libraries on moral or religious grounds: e.g. Israel, Sweden, the Neherlands. Others report that books are so rejected: e.g. Switzerland, Italy, Finland. It is difficult to judge these contradictory experiences. If a school board has the freedom to choose books (whether by way of prescription or recommendation), then it follows that it has the freedom to reject and the question becomes one of how this freedom may be exercised at a given time and place, and how much publicity is given by a free press to controversial dealings and decisions.

The USA provides both controversial cases and healthy attendant publicity. One result of the publicity given in recent years to distinct local cases was to reveal a nationwide trend towards the banning of books from schools, sometimes in a highly irresponsible or emotional manner. In Warsaw, Indiana (not Warsaw, Poland), there was a public burning of books. Some members of school boards took it upon themselves to remove books which were in their eyes "garbage". Others did not bother to read the books through. Victims of similar cleansing operations have included the Dictionary of American Slang and a collection of Best Short Stories by Negro Writers. In Cedar Lake, Indiana, the American Heritage Dictionary was removed from High Schools because it contained among its 135,000 entries 70–80 obscene words. In Louisiana the authorities, aiming to reduce teenage pregnancy, banned a standard biology textbook which explained the human reproductive system too explicitly (believing, apparently, that the sexual urge is intellectual rather than biochemical).

In the widely reported case at Island Trees in Nassau County, N.Y., the school board removed from its schools eleven books which it designated "anti-American, Anti-Christian, anti-semitic and just plain filthy". They included two Pulitzer Prize winners. One of these and one other were later restored. A US District Court ruled that there had been no "sharp and direct" infringement of the First Amendment and that the school board's action fell within "the broad range of discretion" of communally elected local officials. The case is being taken to the Supreme Court on the grounds that the board failed to consider the books as a whole and acted only on the objections of members of the board to extracts.

These examples show that the free circulation of reputable books may be threatened by democracy as well as by authoritarianism. Teachers in the USA report that the demand for the censorship of school books comes overwhelmingly from parents. These may be genuinely worried about what their children are learning or doing at school, or they may be nostalgic reactionaries or just self-important fools; but whatever their motivation the democratic climate of the USA prompts them to form vigilante groups which teachers and school administrators do not always stand up to. In the trade one major supplier has gone so far as to help this kind of censorship by picking out and marking those titles in his catalogues which, on the basis of previous but untested complaints, he considers to be possibly objectionable. By this action he was giving wider circulation undiscriminatingly to valid protest and silly smear; in one case the only objection to the book was that it showed gnomes with no clothes on.

The control over books for schools raises the questions whether, and how far, books intended for children should be more severely controlled than books unlikely to be seen by children; and if so, by whom. The facts are that this form of control is widely regarded as acceptable in some (unspecifiable) degree but that it frequently goes much further in ways which range from the vicious to the silly. The publisher is involved not as *censor morum* but as *Kulturträger*. He is therefore involved in one of those contests about the limits of the permissible which have no end because it is common ground that both permissible and impermissible areas exist and there is no clear line between them. But he is not the umpire in this contest. He is one of the opponents of control. But with certain honourable exceptions—among them some of the big New York houses— he does little about it except observe and bewail. He prefers to keep away from trouble; he regards the controlling authority as a part of the environment to be avoided rather than challenged. The smaller publisher has to be very indignant indeed before he will risk the costs of challenging vicious or fatuous decisions.

But the state's most direct impact on the publisher is to be found in its fiscal functions. The state as taxing authority can hurt the publisher where, increasingly in a period of inflation- and sluggish cash flows, he is most vulnerable: his capacity financially to carry on. The freedom to publish must include the ability to afford to publish. Financial constraints are a bigger obstacle than they were fifty years ago and the publisher who wants to get a decent living out of his business and to avoid having to sell himself into the bondage of a non-publisher proprietor may find himself compelled to reject the worth-while book which he would like to publish and to publish instead more of what he does not esteem. This distortion is certainly a restriction on his freedom, arguably a public disservice. It certainly affects publishing preferences, arguably depresses publishing standards.

Yet it is difficult to lay much of the blame on governmental villainy. Many governments in fact favour books. There is no sales tax on books in, for example, Argentina, Australia, Brazil, Britain, Canada, India, Japan, Mexico, Nigeria, Norway, Spain, Venezuela or Switzerland, although in the last case its imposition is under discusion. In Indonesia particular books may be exempted from tax by the Minister of Education and Culture. It may be that this list should be longer: a number of Associations failed to provide the requisite information. Elsewhere the scale of tax varies considerably. The highest appears to be in Sweden where Value Added Tax (VAT) exceeds 20 per cent. Denmark is a close second with 18 per cent, followed by Finland with 14 per cent. In West Germany, where the standard rate of VAT is 12 per cent, books pay half the rate unless they are included in the list of books harmful to the young. France and Belgium exact 7 and 6 per cent respectively; in France pornography is taxed at 33 per cent. In The Netherlands, where the standard rate of VAT is 18 per cent, the sales price of a book includes a 4 per cent tax. In the USA there is no federal tax on books but the several states or minor localities may impose their own sales taxes and these extend in some areas to books. The tax scene is therefore extremely diverse, with books getting preferential treatment in many countries but not in all.

Authors are almost universally taxed in the same way as individual members of other professions. In Ireland and Israel they enjoy easier terms. In West Germany similar advantages go to authors of scientific works. In Japan, doctors and lawyers enjoy favourable treatment but writers do not. In India, authors may charge a quarter of their earnings or Rs. 5 000, whichever is the less, as expenses before tax.

Taxation of profits (as distinct from sales taxes) raises questions of discrimination in favour of government or official publishing enterprises. In Brazil, Canada, The Netherlands and the USA these do not pay the same taxes as private companies, and the same applies to certain cantonal publishing businesses in Switzerland. This is a more obscure area than such bald statements may imply, since a profit is what is held by an accountant to be a profit and accountancy rules and practices differ not only from country to country but also within countries.

6. Social Constraints and Pressure Groups

The state and the law are not the publisher's only enemies. The law itself is often the easiest of his enemies to identify, to define, and to tilt against. There are even compensating laurels to be won by engaging in a little tilting. But outside the world of one-party or one-man autocracies the law is more a reflection of social norms and values than a tool of arbitrary rules; and it may be criticized, challenged and even changed. Nor is it secret.

Social pressures are another matter. Whereas the law requires obedience to rules which are comparatively precise, social conventions require conformity with canons which are anything but precise. Whereas the law changes overtly at a given moment by the act of a legislative body, conventions change mysteriously and by degrees over time. All that can be said of them in general is that they exist everywhere and that they impose penalties for "going too far". Neither the penalties, nor what is "too far", can be known for certain in advance.

In these respects the publisher is like every other member of society who, wishing to live comfortably within it, needs to understand the society's rules and observe most of them. If he does not like the rules, he may find himself living precariously near the boundaries of his society; or he may choose to overstep the bounds. In either case he runs certain risks and he will think twice before publishing a book which will get him a bad name among people whom he cares about for one reason or another. The social conventions turn him into a self-censor.

Booksellers

The people whom, in this context, he has to bother about are numerous. They include first of all the people who buy the books which he publishes and wishes to sell. These are not in the first instance the members of the public who may read the books but—the book business being constructed as it is—the intermediaries between the publisher and the reader, principally the retail bookseller and the Book Clubs (of whom more below). The bookseller may in effect inhibit the publisher's output, even when no question of legal offence or legal risk arises. With one solitary exception—Norway—no bookseller in any country is under any legal compulsion to take any particular book and offer it for sale: in Norway the bookseller undertakes to take each new book coming from a Norwegian publisher and to stock it for two years. Elsewhere the bookseller weighs not only the book's saleability but also the relevance of its message or its language to contemporary local standards and tastes. If he is himself offended by it, or if he believes that his neighbours and customers will be offended by it, he will not take it.

Libraries

Secondly, there are the libraries, particularly the public libraries financed out of public funds (central or local). Like the bookseller the librarian is under no obligation to acquire a book which he does not like and there are obvious objections to forcing him to do so. Some librarians may be excessively opinionated or squeamish or prejudiced; they may consider that a librarian's duties include the defence of the moral standards which he personally upholds. There is little that the publisher can do except fume and complain that the librarian should never have been appointed in the first place.

Schools

A third area where the publisher may find his book banned by prejudice is, once more, the school. School teachers and school boards have a special standing in relation to the morals of the young within their care. The rules which they apply vary widely and so does their understanding of where youth stops and something less vulnerable begins. In addition, schools run by religious bodies will not unnaturally exclude not merely blasphemous books but also rationally atheistic ones; they seek to regulate beliefs as well as morals. This may, in some people's eyes, be an argument for removing education from sectarian organisations but it is not an argument for preventing those bodies, where they have a teaching role, from deciding for themselves what is wholesome and what is not. It is generally conceded that schools, and particularly religious schools, do censor the publisher's product and normally do so from the highest motives. It is also generally conceded that such censorship is inescapable. Even where a local authority takes power, as in parts of Canada, to insist that a book on (for example) comparative religion must be objective, it will not take power to insist that a particular book shall be used. At most it will limit the choice; it will not direct it.

Pressure groups

The crux here is the vital distinction between public debate and public regulation. Pressure groups have every right to engage in public debate, airing their views and seeking to achieve their aims in this way. When, however, their purpose is to get authority to adopt and enforce their views they enter upon the treacherous grounds labelled "censors at work here". The borderline is not always clear. In Israel, for example, where there is continuing debate between religious bodies and secular bodies such as the League against Religious Coercion, it is not clear whether the former seek to persuade or impose. In Ireland groups such as the Legion of Mary and the Knights of St. Columbanus, self-designated supervisors of the public's morality, comb bookshelves and libraries for material which should in their opinion be banned by the Board of Censors. They are doing no more than what the law allows, but the outcome of their lawful activity is more censorship.

There is another aspect of this problem. Where the bookseller, librarian and teacher may be assumed to be acting in accordance with their own genuine convictions and in the honest exercise of a proper, if private, discretion, the author and publisher have no grounds for complaint. But this is not always the case. Their decisions may have been forced on them by pressure groups who are in the business of making up other people's minds for them.

A pressure group is not as such objectionable. Nobody takes the view that the Anti-Slavery Society should never have been created, and one of the features of democracy is the proliferation of lobbies of one kind or another. Some of these lobbies have aims which other people dislike. Yet others have aims which many people find ridiculous. These are not reasons for suppressing them. Again, some professions form groups to defend their sectional, even selfish, interest and they are entitled to do so. In Britain the Law Society (the solicitors' professional association) took exception to parts of a BBC television programme which were critical of solicitors and pressed for alterations before a second transmission. The BBC refused. Whether in all the circumstances of that case the Law Society was wise to intervene, its right to do so was unassailable. The right of protest is not by itself a form of censorship.

Lobbyists

More difficult cases arise where a group is formed not to defend its own members but to propagate a set of ideas or to stifle contrary ideas. It is neither necessary, nor in most cases, plausible to assume that these lobbyists or propagandists are anything but sincere, nor should they be denied the right to associate and propagate. Yet it is also undeniable that their greatest triumphs occur when they induce other people to do what they have not wished to do—if only because, had they so wished, they would have done so already and without any effort on the part of the lobbyists. The means employed to achieve these triumphs are not always admirable. When persuasion goes beyond argument and calls in aid either moral blackmail or the support of prominent personages because they are prominent, with the aim of bringing social or commercial pressures to bear, then the world of the pressure groups loses much of its respectability. And the publisher is faced with the problem whether to submit or not. He is then no longer consulting his own conscience but weighing the pros and cons of acceding to somebody else's.

In deciding what to do he will be guided by his own temperament and prejudices—and also by the sheer cost of resisting a powerful or persistent group. In a recent case in Britain the Festival of Light, a body created to uphold certain beliefs and codes of conduct, tried to prevent the firm of W. H. Allen from publishing *The Sexual Outlaw,* a book which is in effect a defence of homosexuality. The publisher, who had 4,500 copies of the book in print, had to choose between bowing to the pressures brought against him or incurring considerable extra expenditure on lawyers, psychologists and "literary experts". The publisher chose the latter course and the pressures faded away; he held his ground and prevailed. But a less determined or less principled publisher might have chosen otherwise, and a small publisher would have been bound to jib at the expense. The conclusion is that pressure groups have some power to stop publications, provided they select the right publishers to harass: those of weak will or thin purses. Resistance requires firm conviction and a bank balance.

This power of the pressure group is derived from the forces of social convention and conformity. No less than the law, the social and moral climate in which the publisher operates circumscribes his freedom. He is constrained by his natural distaste for making himself disagreeable or conspicuous. Clearly this does not apply to those publishers who positively enjoy making themselves disagreeable or conspicuous, either from innate cussedness or showmanship or because their righteous indignation carries them over the bounds of conformity and prudence and what the majority judges to be good taste. But it may be surmised, without the need for rigorous research, that most publishers come from the conformist ranks of their society or the merely mildly non-conformist. Traditionally they have been liberally-minded men of letters or the sons of such, readier to permit than themselves to perpetrate anything outrageous, and where this type of middle class publisher is now giving ground to interlopers from the financial world, the newcomers who buy their way into publishing are likely to be even more decidedly conformist and conservative; they are readier to applaud adventures in investment than in ideas. By nature they uphold the social norms and are at best lukewarm in their support of colleagues who do not. Most publishers therefore are not offering to the book trade or the public much that either sees cause to repugn. Consequently these publishers have few complaints about the matters reviewed in this section and it is not surprising that their representative Associations report, virtually unanimously and often monosyllabically, that on this front all is well.

There remains the minority, for whom the conventions are a restraint which they resent and wish to reduce. Formally they are almost everywhere (outside dictatorships and juntas and even, by the letter of the law, within many of them) free to question, for example, conventional ideas about sex and marriage, to question the "truths" of the prevailing religion and to promote a rival one. Yet there are limits, distinct from the limits set by the law, and entailing penalties unknown to the law. If, as the Norwegian Association reports, theirs is "a very puritanical people" the publisher must live and work with this fact. And no doubt up to a point he should. What is irksome is, first, that when tempted to challenge the norms he should be restrained by the cost of doing so; and, secondly, that a number of pressure groups become so obsessed by the righteousness of their ends that they employ dubious means to reach them.

7. The Takeover of Publishing

We have reviewed some of the obstacles which are placed by the state and the law in the way of the publisher's freedom to publish what he pleases. We have also reviewed the different obstacles which society and its pressure groups impose. These are the obstacles which first spring to mind when the question of the publisher's freedom is raised. They have been for centuries, and still are, characteristic of unstable societies and of rigorously conservative ones, but broadly speaking they are neither conspicuous nor endemic in firmly established liberal democracies such as are the norm in Western Europe and North America. But these societies have no cause for complacency, for their publishers face threats to freedom which are potentially even more serious because they may well be irreversible.

These threats emerge from the changing structure, particularly the changing financial structure, of the world of books. Within this area are two distinct issues which form the subject matter of this and the next section of this report. The first is the transfer of the ownership of publishing businesses from publishers to non-publishers. The second is the transformation of book distribution, particularly the partial displacement of the retail bookseller by the Book Club. Both these trends—but most notably the first—import into publishing the most dangerous interference with the publisher's independence since the invention of printing gave him a key role in a liberal culture.

Independent publishers

The freedom of the publisher to publish what he wishes is negated in the most elementary sense when he ceases to be master in his own house. This situation is becoming increasingly common. The acquisition of a publishing business by non-publishers has many aspects but only one broad conclusion. It reverses ends and means in publishing.

The publisher's central aim is to publish books; money is a necessary means to this end. But for the non-publisher who buys a publishing business the end is money; publishing is one of the means. This is a qualitative difference and, technical changes apart, it constitutes the most profound mutation that has ever occurred in the history of publishing.

The eclipse of the independent publisher began when he first sold a share in his business to somebody else. In practice a sleeping partner with a minor share makes little difference and such adjuncts have been around in publishing for a hundred years or more. The next stage came with the sale of shares to the public at large. Even when the publisher retains control he feels obliged to consider the purely material interests of the outside shareholders and therefore to worry about the ups and downs of his company's quotation on the stock exchange. The publisher who begins the day by turning to the city pages of the newspaper is half way to becoming something other than a publisher. But the practical limits on the powers of a dispersed body of share holders are well known; they rarely understand or interfere. The big change comes when the publisher sells a share in his business not to the public at large but to a single purchaser—the more so since the purchaser in a transaction of this kind normally requires control. The publisher has then sunk to the level of employee of a non-publisher.

Before doing this a number of publishers have sought to fend off outside bids through amalgamations among themselves. In the USA there have been some 200 mergers in 10 years and over 80 per cent of the paperback market is now supplied by a mere 8 publishers. In France, it has been calculated, something like 90 per cent of the paperback market is controlled by 10 publishers. This trend is sometimes cited as an evil in its own right even though it cannot yet be said to have reached monopolistic proportions. More to the point of the present inquiry is the fact that such amalgamations are as likely to accelerate as to block the incursions of outside purchasers since, by grouping firms by merger, they make it possible for a purchaser to buy several firms in one swoop.

Non-publishers

The invasion of publishing by non-publishers which developed during the 60's and 70's into a veritable scramble for such properties was caused by the appetites of these new proprietors. No financier would buy a publishing business unless he thought it a "good buy" and likely to produce attractive profits. If his accountants did not advise him that the purchase was financially sound, he would remain blind to publishing's other attractions and stay away. This is not to say that the publisher for his part is always, or violently, averse to being bought. He may be in, or may anticipate, such difficulties that he has to choose between selling his business to an outsider and watching it decline and fail. It is nevertheless a fair generalization that the great majority of publishers sell themselves only under financial constraint and that they prefer in these circumstances to join forces with another publisher rather than deliver themselves over to non-publishers.

The non-publisher proprietor is by definition ignorant of publishing and in consequence incapable, or at least severely handicapped, when it comes to making publishing judgements. He may too be relatively unacquainted with books and spend little of his time reading them. He is probably remote from the business which he has bought and has to work hard to win the loyalty which is commonly accorded to expertise or acquired by working at close quarters with colleagues. He does not as a rule begin by displacing those who have been running the business but sooner or later he will exercise his right to appoint non-publishers to the publishing board and may even constitute a board on which publishers are in a minority to imported accountants, "managers" or "executives" many of them part-time pluralists for ever on the move from one board room to another.

At this point the change in ownership begins to make a significant impact on the publisher's list. Publishers think first and foremost about books and about the future. Their principal concern is to get new books. A number of them have done this to the exclusion of good commercial management, for which a literary flair is certainly no substitute. These have in consequence gone to the wall—which, however, is their own funeral, self-induced. They may be lamented by their brethren but they can hardly claim to be rescued from their myopia. If they are replaced by a board of non-publishers with harder heads on their shoulder, that is no bad thing for publishing. Yet other dangers arise, not only different but potentially more serious. The new directors, who too frequently do not know how to get books or judge them, concentrate instead on statistics and therefore on the past—on the "performance" (to use the jargon) or books already published. For such a board the main indicator of success is last quarter's set of figures rather than next season's list of new titles. This reversal of values may even go to the lengths of relegating the discussion of books to an inferior group or committee. Publishing judgements are downgraded.

Furthermore the publisher who has become the employee of non-publishers will in some degree, consciously or unconsciously, give heed to his employer's tastes as well as to his natural preoccupation with the return on the investment which he made when he bought the business. These tastes may not be seriously or frequently different from the publisher's own tastes, and when they do differ who is to say that the publisher is right and the proprietor wrong? The publisher is not a superior being (either spiritually or intellectually), nor is the proprietor a villain. But the publisher, though not superior, is different; in the difference lies part of his usefulness; and this difference will be at its strongest with the type of publisher who, not without benefit to the community over the ages, has chosen to push at the boundaries of current taste and behaviour. Sooner or later this publisher will want to publish a book which makes the new proprietor uneasy. The proprietor does not relish being chaffed in his own world for his responsibility for a book which his circle finds offensive. So one day one such book will be rejected. Publishing is stunted.

In expressing their reactions to this mutation publishers vary. A number of them acknowledge that things have hardly changed with the takeover. But even the more optimistic are inclined to add: Not yet. The change is fundamental even where its manifestations are delayed. Moreover a first takeover, negotiated by the publisher with a known purchaser, may be followed by a second in which the first purchaser sells the business to a second purchaser without being obliged to get the original publisher's consent. The publisher who sells himself once is therefore alienating not merely his independence but his right to have a say in whom he is to be dependent upon.

Even the financial inducement—the original *quid* proquo which sweetened the bartering of independence—may fail. The strongest argument in favour of a takeover is that the publisher, seeing his cash flow reduced to a trickle, needs the financial backing which a powerful financier can supply. But cases have occurred where the new proprietor, so far from sustaining his publishing business in hard times, presses it to generate more cash for him. What the proprietor has promised to provide he now asks for, and this reverse-aid not only negates the publisher's financial expectations but also constrains him to alter the balance of his list in order to maximize cash flow for somebody else's benefit. The pattern of his publishing is no longer settled by publishing expertise and criteria but by financial considerations which obtrude themselves from outside. In particular, the more volatile book is preferred to the more serious and—to the ultimate detriment of the list—to the book with the longer expectation of life; and a larger share of the publisher's resources has to be allocated to reprints rather than new books. The essential point is that these decisions flow not from the publisher's assessments but from the proprietor's needs. The publisher's freedom is eroded and publishing as a whole is damaged.

It is impossible to quantify the shift of publishing businesses into alien ownership. Reliable statistics of the extent of this takeover exist neither in terms of the number of businesses acquired, nor in terms of the volume of publishing whether measured by turnover or by the number of titles published.

Publishers might be well advised to take stock and assemble such figures. But the trend is evident and in some countries—notably the USA and Britain—massive as finance houses and other conglomerates move into a hitherto neglected zone and appropriate chunks of it. Some of these invaders have what they call compatible interests: e.g. broadcasting and television corporations (among them RCA and CBS in the USA, Granada Television and London Weekend Television in Britain) or newspaper publishers (the Hearst Corporation, Thomson International, S. Pearson and Co). Others (ITT, Gulf and Western, Mattel, Tillings) have much more tenuous connections with the world of books, although it does not follow that they therefore inflict more injury on publishing or even that, in a particular case, they inflict any injury at all. But the fact is that, in the USA for example, a handful of alien corporations has bought a dozen of the more prestigious publishing houses and that here as elsewhere these corporations have chosen book publishing for no discernible reason other than the belief that this is a field in which their money can be put to financially fruitful use. A number of European countires—France, Italy, Sweden—reflect the same process, although yet others—Denmark, Norway, West Germany—remain as yet relatively unaffected. The process seems likely to spread ever further. The 70's have all the appearance of a period of transition whose varieties can be observed in microcosm in Scandinavia. In Denmark Gyldendal, almost a national institution, stands firmly independent. In Norway leading publishers are still their own masters. In Finland, major businesses have passed into multiple ownership, albeit that the new proprietors operate mainly in allied trades. In Sweden the equivalent firms have been acquired by proprietors who are mainly involved in activities which have nothing to do with books.

But whatever the local differences, and whatever the statistics might show, one fact is clear and significant: whereas the takover of publishers by non-publishers is now in publishing terms substantial, the involvement of non-publishers in publishing is in their own terms marginal.

On all these counts the role which the independent publisher has played in liberal societies over the past four of five centuries is being occluded and it is not alarmist to pose the question how he may survive as more and more publishing territory is taken over by persons and corporations with alien interests, alien outlooks and alien values.

8. The Distributive Trade

The publisher is a middle-man. Inevitably he is to some extent dependent on those who distribute his books, unless he undertakes the whole business of distribution himself. The question which arises in the context of this report is whether this dependence has created, or seems likely to create, a situation in which the publisher's freedom to fashion his own list is materially affected by distributors.

Distributors are in no position to affect the publisher's freedom to publish what he wants unless they secure a monopolistic or near-monopolistic position or organize an effective cartel. Where, however, they do secure such a position they may acquire an influence over the publisher, direct or indirect: direct if they refuse to handle a particular book, indirect if the publisher feels obliged to reject a book or to re-cast the balance of his list in the light of what he believes distributors' wishes to be.

By and large the freedom to publish is not at present impeded either by the retail bookseller or by the chains which deal in books. It is very difficult to discover instances where the publisher has made his decision to publish conditional upon getting a favourable response from distributors. What can be said with fair certainty is that there are a few books which the publisher does not wish to publish unless he can be assured of an exceptionally big sale and that in such cases he will defer his acceptance of the book until he has taken soundings among the main distributors. But if he chooses to act in this way, he can hardly be heard to complain that his freedom is being interferred with, for if he then decides not to publish, that is his own decision. Taking soundings is not to be equated with *force majeure*.

Traditionally publishers have formed an alliance with the retail book trade. At the core of this alliance was the net book agreement which, in various forms in different countries, allowed the publisher to dictate to the bookseller and so to the public the price at which the book should be sold. The price paid by publishers to the retail trade for this privilege and control was to vest in the retail trade a virtual monopoly of the sale of books to the public. The publisher fixed prices and agreed in return not to supply books—or not to supply them at regular trade discounts—to any retailer who could not get admittance to a booksellers' association. (The exceptions are well known and need not be detailed here.) Thus publishers and booksellers together controlled the trade, including the creation of new outlets.

From the publishers' point of view this system was vulnerable in two ways. It offended those who disapprove of price fixing and it contained a hidden weakness if the day should come when, within this closed system, the distributors became more powerful than the publishers.

On the first of these issues publishers have defended net book agreements on the grounds that, however much the price fixing element may seem to disadvantage the public, ultimately the maintenance of a retail book trade distinct from general retail trade is in the public interest and can be secured in no other way. The arguments are, once again, too well known to need repetition. They triumphed in a famous case in Britain in

1962 but the fact is that they have been losing ground and net book agreements have been breaking down. Even the compromise of a "recommended" price, used for example in Australia, has been made illegal in some countries. Between 1970, when price fixing was made illegal in the book trade in Sweden, and 1979, when it was abandoned in France, the 70's have seen a progressive erosion of protectionism.

This erosion has coincided with a trend towards larger units in the retail trade. In the past bookselling has typically been in the hands of a large number of small businesses. In spite of the existence of a few larger businesses and chains which have combined bookselling with newspapers, magazines and stationery, the book trade has been fragmented and so relatively powerless—a fact which has helped to preserve the dominance of the publisher in the publisher-bookseller alliance. A shift towards larger and fewer units in the trade potentially threatens this dominance and so the publisher's ability to construct his list independently of the wishes or tastes of distributors. But the trend must not be exaggerated. Amalgamations and acquisitions within the trade have not so far created anything approaching a monopoly. In Britain the most conspicuous distributor—W. H. Smith—handles 20 % of the paperback trade and rather more than 10 % of the hardback trade. The refusal therefore of a single distributor to sell a particular book is no more than a nuisance; it could not entitle a publisher to reject a book and lay the blame on the distributor. (There is always the possibility that a major distributor's refusal to handle a book may, if properly exploited, increase the attention given to a book and its sales. So may the mere attempt to get booksellers to boycott a book. In 1976 the French government allegedly tried to prevent the distribution in its ex-colonies of *Les confettis de l'empire* by Jean Guillebord, a book which described the last phase of colonialism. The government did not go so far as to invoke the law against the publishers and did succeed in giving the book much extra publicity.)

Yet there is some alarm among publishers. The power of Hachette in France is a favourite example of dangers ahead. Through its virtual monopoly of outlets at railway stations, airports and news stands, Hachette are in a position to decide what books shall or shall not be offered to the substantial section of bookbuyers who use these outlets. But even this exceptionally pervasive control does not amount to, or even approximate to, a nationwide monopoly in the book trade as a whole, and even in France it remains true to say that if a publisher declines to publish a book through fear of the distributors, he is less a victim than a coward.

It would be a mistake to suppose that distributors deliberately set out to use such power as they have in order to regulate the publisher's pattern of publishing. They are more immediately interested in the terms upon which they deal with the publisher than in the contents of his books. In so far as this concern is a threat to the publisher it is a threat to his profits and, secondarily, a curb on the quality of his list; it is not a threat to his independent existence. By demanding higher discounts and other favours the distributor with adequate commercial muscle presses the publisher into a corner. (It was apparently this kind of conflict which led Gallimard in 1970 to break its association with Hachette and establish its own distribution network as well as its new pocket book series.) Some books can be published profitably in spite of increased demands by distributors; others not. Faced therefore with demands which he feels compelled to meet the publisher will publish more of the former and fewer of the latter—which are the "better" or more serious works or books with only a minority appeal. Publishing in these areas will shrink, while the distributors shelves fill up with anti-books such as TV scripts and tie-ins, concocted and designed (if that is not too artistic a description) to sell in huge numbers to semi-literates. The central question for publishers is how far catering for these requirements, which will not cease, destroys or seriously damages the publisher's ability to find outlets for the kind of book which he wishes to publish and believes himself to be in business to publish. This is a very large socio-economic question. The commonest response is one of passive pessimism. Thoughtful publishers do not like the look of the world they are about to live in. One of the reasons is that they see the retail book business sliding into the zone described in the last section, where money is not servant but king.

Book clubs

Whether by chance, logic or design these trends in the book trade have coincided in the seventies with the accelerating rise of an alternative to it: the Book Club. The Book Club has been the salvation of a number of publishers, but it is also seen as a threat. It has been a salvation by providing sales by mail order techniques where sales through booksellers have been flagging; in some cases Book Clubs picked up what booksellers were losing, in others they found a new market. In Sweden, for example, where publishers had a bad time in the early seventies, Book Clubs saved them from having a worse time. In Norway publishers acknowledge unequivocally that without Book Club sales they would not have been able to keep financially afloat. In a number of countries a publisher has been enabled to re-issue a worthwhile out-of-print book only because a Book Club has come along with an offer to take a few thousand copies.

But the obverse of this development is the fear that Book Clubs are acquiring an unhealthy dominance over publishing. By becoming financially important they impinge on publishing choices. By virtue of their success they are an aid to the publisher's livelihood but, by the same token, a threat to the diversity and quality of his publishing.

Book Clubs are very various. Some sell to their members books which have been on sale in bookshops for a significant period. Others offer new books contemporaneously with their first appearance in the shops. In Sweden, to take a single example, the Book of the Month Club owned jointly by Bonniers and Norstedt offers new books, whereas Norstedt's Family Book Club offers monthly a single new book at the head of a catalogue which lists a large number and variety of stock titles and which is in effect a specialised mail order catalogue. Again, some Clubs are specific while others are general. The former aims at a specialised group of readers which may be fairly wide—a history Book Club—or decidedly restricted—a Club for specialists in the uniforms and military insignia of World War II. These are very clubby Clubs. The general Club on the other hand is hardly a Club at all. It has no limits to its subject matter. Like the general bookseller it offers a bit of everything, or a lot of everything, to everybody.

The general Book Club aims at the widest attainable membership, and this is what matters in the context of this report. The existence of a specific Book Club has only negligible effects on the publisher's planning of his list; the publisher treats a "choice" by such a Club as a pleasant bonus but does not make it a test of whether to publish a book or not. But the big general Club is, or may become, a different matter. There comes a point where the benefits measured in money or publicity or author-satisfaction, so seduce the publisher that he will devote a disproportionate amount of time and effort to chasing these benefits, or try to re-fashion a book in order to give it a better chance of hooking them. The financial success of a list may even come to depend on securing a couple of juicy choices year after year. Again, it might seem to the purist to be more appropriate to blame the publisher for letting himself and his list be manipulated in this way, but whether publisher or Book Club is to blame it remains true that considerations of this kind are increasingly imposing themselves on publishing judgements and tactics.

Sweden

The country where the enrolment of Book Club members has gone furthest (as a proportion of total population) appears to be Sweden, where sales through Swedish Book Clubs have reached 40 % of the total volume. This explosion began at the time of the abrogation of the Swedish net book agreement in 1970 and has led to fierce competition between the Clubs owned by rival publishers. (In Norway on the other hand, leading publishers established jointly a single Club run by a distinct company owned by the publishers but operated independently.) Swedish booksellers have responded by forming regional associations which offer to take large numbers of a few selected titles in return for larger discounts—a response which not only cuts the publisher's profits per copy on those titles but further concentrates attention and effort on a few titles at the expense of the rest. Thus the booksellers, under the impact of the rivalry of the Book Clubs, have joined in the trend to narrow the market.

West Germany

But the example which most publishers have in mind is not Scandinavian but German. In West Germany—and now beyond it—Bertelsmann has built up a general Book Club of such dimensions that it may claim to provide Bertelsmann's customers with every kind of book and, through its mail order catalogues, spare them the trouble of going to a bookshop. With six million subscribers in West Germany and (assuming 2.5 readers for every volume sent to a member) a reading circle embracing a quarter of the population Bertelsmann bids fair to become a novel cultural force. It has planned to extend its activities into 20 other countries. It has a turnover, from books alone, double that which the largest U.S. publisher derives from books, magazines and other activities. It scares publishers. Yet the number of books which it distributes in its home territory is still a minor part of the total sale of books in West Germany and the pace of its expansion has, whether temporarily or not, been restrained in the last year or two.

It is not easy to distinguish how far dislike of these phenomena is economic and how far it is cultural. In one sense the Book Clubs are the descendants of the lending libraries of an earlier age. But in another sense they reverse the role of the libraries. The libraries provided facilities for a reading public with a fair idea of what it wanted to read but no easy way to get it. The Book Club provides books for a wider and widening public which wants to read but does not on the whole know what. The Book Club, while ostensibly offering its members a "choice", is itself making the choices and so telling readers what to read. This sort of direction is offensive to the traditional literary classes who see it as a species of mind control, albeit exercised not to win power but to make money. How far this revulsion is commendable is a question which lies outside the scope of this report.

But the economic consequences, and the economic anxieties of publishers, are real. Bertelsmann may be all but unique at present but it will not remain so, and a colossus of this kind, monopolizing the attention and directing the taste of a substantial section of the reading public, understandably worries publishers who have been used to a variegated and fragmented retail trade in which they have held more power than the distributors of their wares. The rise of the Book Club threatens their ascendancy and puts the publisher in a dilemma.

It does so in two ways. Some publishers are directly dependent on Book Clubs. Without straying from West Germany we may instance S. Fischer and Rohwolt, whose survival has been assured by Book Clubs. Further afield Heinemann and Collins are launching a new Club with Bonniers. Secondly, the Book Club has been increasingly taking the place of the bookshop by catering by direct mail for a new reading public which does not go into bookshops and cannot yet find books in sufficient quantities in supermarkets. This alliance of the economic power of the extended reading public and of the Book Club operator is forcing the publisher to attend to their amalgamated wishes—which are in effect largely the wishes of the latter. The publisher can hardly afford to restrict his business to the older and mainly middle class public and its traditional outlet, the bookshop. But some of the changes in the nature of the book trade—in response to rises in literacy and the reading habit—are deeply unpalatable. They threaten to convert publishing into a competition for the favours of a special type of big buyer, the Book Club—a revival in secular guise of the need for the *imprimatur*. And, secondly, in seeking these favours the publisher is propelled towards trivializing, cosmeticizing and (in the pejorative sense) vulgarizing a product which he is then tempted to oversell by the cruder and not always honest methods of modern marketeers. This is a second *trahison des clercs*. What suffers is the culturally worthier book, the book published for a small minority and above all new fiction. The last of these categories is probably the most vulnerable, as a final illustration will demonstrate. At Norstedt in Stockholm sales of new serious fiction through Book Clubs now run at the level of a third to one half of the sales of the same books through the trade. The dependence of this kind of publishing on Book Clubs is therefore pronounced and like all kinds of dependence unwelcome. The publisher foresees himself being forced to abandon or at least severely restrict one of his most cherished services.

Note on professional regulations

Freedom to publish may be restricted if the right to publish is confined to membership of a professional body in the way in which many commercial activities were limited in the Middle Ages by vesting a monopoly in a narrow and self-perpetuating group. Nowadays no professional association has the right or the means to prevent non-members from setting up as publishers and there is no obligation on a publisher to join a professional body. Such at any rate is the unanimous report of the I.P.A's member Associations.

One member Association only has reported the existence of conditions which have to be fulfilled before a publisher may join his country's Association. In Norway a publisher has to be in business for three years before he becomes eligible for membership. There is similar unanimity in the replies concerning government interference in the affairs of a Publishers

Association. No association feels that there is any such interference. The very question seems shocking.

Bookselling is in most countries equally open to all insofar as there are no special legal obstacles and no professional requirement to join an association. Where, as for example in Italy, a retailer or a wholesaler has to be licensed before he may engage in trade, this requirement applies to a bookseller as much as to any other kind of tradesman.

In parts of Scandinavia publishers go somewhat further. In Norway the bookseller must show three years of experience in bookselling and provide financial guarantees. In Denmark the more expensive books (40 Kr. and above) may be sold only by booksellers judged by the Publishers Association to have the requisite training and skills; substantially this means that an aspiring bookseller must first do a stint as a bookseller's assistant.

Composed with Baskerville 10/13 and
printed on TF Bokpapper from Klippanbruken
and Tre Kronor from Tumba
by Almqvist & Wiksell, Uppsala, Sweden 1980.
Typographic design by Dick Hallström
and cover design by Per-Ivar Glaser